Two Villages

And The

Great War

D P Clifford FRSC

British Library Cataloguing in Publication Data.
A catalogue record for this book is available from the British Library

ISBN 978 0 86071 794 2

A Commissioned Publication Printed by

MOORLEYS
Print, Design & Publishing
info@moorleys.co.uk · www.moorleys.co.uk

ACKNOWLEDGEMENTS

I would like to thank local people, particularly those of the congregations of the two churches, far too many to name, who helped with 'local knowledge'. Especial thanks to Mr John Blant, Mrs Kathy Blant and Mrs Marion Henshell for providing and allowing the use of many of the photographs included.

Where possible attribution is given to the source of photographs.

For a few of the photographs for which I do not have a source: my thanks to the people for their generosity in donating them for use in various exhibitions which have lead to them being used here: without them some of the ambience and colour that I have tried to convey about the villages would have been lost.

FOREWORD

This book attempts to find out about the men of military age from the villages of Bilborough and Strelley who went to fight in WW1, the Great War.

All readers who have attempted to trace their family genealogy will know of the difficulties in firstly, identifying a person and then making certain that the individual found was indeed the person being sought. Surnames such as Smith can provide insurmountable hurdles, since there will be so many records. What is required is a whole series of refining terms to narrow down the number: the name of a husband or wife, a place of birth, a particular occupation etc. The whole may further be complicated by missing or destroyed records. In searching the histories, civilian and military, of 135 men provides the additional complication of volume.

Many military records were destroyed after the First World War: the failure to find a record therefore did not mean that the individual did not serve. The villages produced a 'Roll of Honour' book. This book covers only those men who were resident in the village at some time during the war. Of the 40 men recorded only 22 were living in the village in 1911, according to the census of that year. Each man has a page, and in some cases two, on which their war record was recorded. Some pages record only the name and regiment joined. The source of the information for each man is not stated. It presumably came from the man himself, possibly family or friends. In the case of those who lost their lives, the latter would have been the only source. What the book contains, that is almost impossible to get elsewhere, are the battles and experiences that the individual men were involved in.

The names of those men of military, or potentially military, age in the 1911 census, with those in the Roll of Honour book, gave 135 males who would be of an age to serve during 1914-1918. Some of these men clearly moved out of the villages subsequent to 1911, since they are not recorded in the book. However in some cases their families continued to live in the villages during and after the war. They were therefore included here and their details included in the Appendices.

After comprehensive searches covering a number of databases, details were found for many of the men but not necessarily a war record. Searching sources for 135 men generated a great deal of data and a large volume of statistics, which for some would be of great importance but which others would find too dry and possibly boring. For this reason tables of complete details of particular aspects, as they are touched upon, have been included as appendices. The fleshing out of the lives and possible characters of the men involved (occasionally with photographs) and the conclusions drawn are presented in the first part of the book with as little in the way of numerical detail included as possible.

To find out something about the lives of the people the following sources were used:
-census records
-records of birth, deaths and marriages
-electoral rolls
-1939 Register

-military records
-Roll of Honour book
-Edge estate books
-newspaper articles of the time
-local church exhibitions on the subject
-local oral history

From time to time other parishes are mentioned. To enable the reader to follow the movement of people from local parish to parish, a sketch map of Strelley, Bilborough and their surrounding parishes can be found as Fig. 1.

Bibliographical references are included at the end of the appropriate phrase, or sentence, and, if numerical, are placed in parentheses.

Fig. 1 Map showing the surrounding parishes of Bilborough and Strelley

LIST OF FIGURES

LIST OF TABLES

LIST OF APPENDICES

INTRODUCTION

Much has been written on the Great War of 1914-1918, its causes, the great battles, the leading personalities, both politicians and generals. It can be reduced to statistics, 50 billion bullets, 1 billion artillery shells, 1 million machine guns, tens of millions dead and even more wounded.

These statistics bring home the magnitude of the conflict. Photographs and film of the time reflect some of the horror experienced by those involved on the front line. The Great War affected the lives of people across the world and particularly in Europe. The lives of people in Britain were to change forever as a result of the war in terms of the carnage, some destruction of their cities and the changes in society that the war brought about, not to mention the grief that it brought to many families.

The statistics, however, do not fully represent the grief and effect on people's lives. It was Stalin who said "kill a million people and it is a statistic. Give one a name and it is a tragedy".

On the memorial to the dead of these two small villages, Fig. 2, are four names: their loss a tragedy for their families and friends. But who were they and what were they like? For the many that went some returned physically wounded and mentally scarred. Even if they survived, the experience would alter their lives and those of their families. This book seeks to find out about the lives, not only of those who died but of all who went to fight in the Great War. In doing so to try and piece together their lives, before, during and after the war, and to give some insight as to what it was to be them and those like them, during those times. In short, to give a name to a statistic and if possible a face to a name, and to better understand the tragedy for them, their families and the villages as a whole.

It is appropriate perhaps to start with the memorial erected in Strelley village to the four men, from both villages, who died in the Great War, Fig.2.

In addition to the Calvary memorial a Roll of Honour book was produced in 1920 which listed the 40 men, of both villages, who died or served. A large framed scroll, produced by the same calligrapher who produced the Roll of Honour book, is hung in St. Martin's church, listing just the men from Bilborough. A memorial chapel was built in the south transept, of Strelley All Saints church, in 1927, as a memorial to the wife of the then squire T L K Edge. The board dedicating it to her is also dedicated to the men of the village who served in the war.

THE VILLAGES

The adjacent villages of Bilborough and Strelley in 1914 were independent villages, with Nottingham the nearest large city. The city's boundaries have now subsumed Bilborough and crept up to that of the parish of Strelley. Both of the villages are mentioned in the Doomsday book. Over the years they would have grown with cottages clustered around the village church with farmhouses scattered around the parish. This was certainly true of Bilborough (see 1911 census map, Fig. 10) and originally true of Strelley. The Edge family took over the estates covering the two parishes, from the Strelley family in 1678, and lived in Strelley Hall. At the end of the 18thC, Thomas Webb Edge, knocked down the houses around the Hall and the church. He rebuilt them c. ½ mile away, to the south east, out of sight of the Hall, on the boundary of the two parishes, which allowed him to create an open parkland setting for the Hall.

The churches of the two villages are medieval. Restoration of that of Strelley, All Saints, Fig. 3, was begun in 1356 from the remains of a church believed to be 12thC. It was begun by Sir Sampson de Strelley in grateful thanks for his being spared the Black Death and completed near the end of that century.

The church of Bilborough, St. Martin of Tours, is also medieval and, despite some architectural butchery of the 1950s, has been carefully and sympathetically restored as near as possible to its original condition, Fig. 4. These two churches would have been at the centre of the lives of many of the serving men and their photographs reflect some of the peace of the villages in the early years of the twentieth century. They were served by the same rector after the Civil War and were formally united in 1838.

In 1911 (from the census) the population of Bilborough was 202 (106 male) and that of Strelley 198 (97 male). In comparison, in 2016, the population of Bilborough was c.16,000 and that of Strelley, in 2012, 640.

The early twentieth century was an era when a few people owned most of the assets. In Nottinghamshire the five largest landowners owned 27% of the acres: the Dukes of Portland and Newcastle; Earl Manvers; Lord Middleton and A W Savile. On a smaller scale, but in the same vein, the lands of the parishes were owned by the powerful Edge family, who dominated both parishes. Many of the population worked directly or indirectly for them and many lived in tied cottages. They lived in Strelley Hall, Fig. 5.

Fig. 2 Memorial, in Strelley churchyard, to the fallen of the Great War

Fig. 3 All Saints Church, Strelley

Fig. 4 St. Martin of Tours Church, Bilborough

Fig. 5 An early image of Strelley Hall

In the Roll of Honour book, previously mentioned, there is no obvious way of knowing whether all of the men of the village who served were included and what or who was the source of the information included. For several of the men, all that is entered is their name and regiment: these men (and their families) may at some point during the war, or immediately after, have moved elsewhere. They were therefore not available to provide the details of the places served, wounds suffered and various dates. It is likely that the men themselves provided much of the information with some coming from family and friends: this must have been the case for those killed. It is probable that, given the unreliability of memory, some of the information, particularly dates, is not accurate. For some the need to embellish and the self deprecation of others may have coloured their accounts. In all the names of 40 are included. As mentioned earlier the number swells to a potential of 135 when the men of military age, listed in the Census of 1911, between 1914 and 1918 are included.

Military records were found for a further 30 men making 70 in total. These 30 were either omitted from the Roll of Honour book or had moved out of the villages over the next 3 to 7 years and whose details could possibly be included elsewhere. For some, their families still lived in Strelley or Bilborough and it was considered appropriate that they be considered along with the 40 in the Roll of Honour book.

It is interesting to note that only those men who joined as officers received British medals for gallantry: three received the Military Cross. John Henry Booth who joined in the ranks and rose to become an officer, was given an Italian medal for gallantry, but no British medal. To help with ranks, of the British Army, as you read the book, see Table 1, with medals for gallantry and campaign medals, Table 2.

All men that served received campaign medals. These were the 1915 Star, the British Army Medal and the Victory Medal known facetiously, at the time, as "Pip, Squeak and Wilfred". Most of the men who fought would have received the latter two, but only those who served in 1914 and 1915, before 'Conscription', received the first.

CONDITIONS OF LIFE IN 1914

The living conditions of a century ago were very different to those of today. "The good old days" were definitely not so when the detail of how people had to live is examined. It is worth taking a little time to look at those conditions to give the general background of life as experienced nationally, as well as by the people of Strelley and Bilborough. This will give some idea of the lives that they were living before the war, and give some insight as to why they might have decided to join up.

TABLE 1. MILITARY RANKS

Rank	No. of Men commanded	Name
Field Marshal	2,000,000	
General	300,000	Army
Lt. General	60,000	Corps
Major General	12,000	Division
Brigadier General	3,500	Brigade
Lt. Colonel	1,000	Battalion
Major		Battalion, 2nd in command
Captain	200	Company
Lt./2nd Lt.	50	Platoon
Sergeant		Platoon, 2nd in command
Corporal/L/Corporal	12	Section
Private	0	

Source: British Library. bl.uk/worldwar-one

Campaign or War medals awarded for service outside UK in the Theatre of War at the time of the war. These were awarded to all ranks.

1914 Star. For those who served in France or Belgium 05/08/1914 to 11/11/1918
1914-1915 Star. For service in theatre of war 05/08/1914 to 31/12/1915
British War Medal. All who served 05/08/1914 to 11/11/1918
The Allied Victory Medal. Not all who received the British War Medal received this.
Territorial Force War Medal 1914-1919
Silver War Badge
Mercantile Marine War Medal

TABLE 2. MEDALS OF 1914-1918
Gallantry medals in order of precedence

Medal	Awarded to
Victoria Cross, VC	All ranks
Distinguished Service Order, DSO	Officers
Distinguished Service Cross, DSC	Officers
Military Cross, MC	Officers
Distinguished Flying Cross, DFC	Officers
Airforce Flying Cross, AFC	Officers
Distinguished Conduct Medal, DCM	Other ranks. Equivalent to DSO
Conspicuous Gallantry Medal, CGM	Other ranks. Equivalent to DCM
Distinguished Service Medal, DSM	Other ranks. Equiv. to MM, DFM, AFM
Military Medal, MM	Other ranks. Equiv. to DCM, DFM, AFM
Distinguished Flying Medal, DFM	Other ranks. Equiv. to DFM, MM, AFM
Air Force Medal, AFM	All ranks
Meritorious Service Medal, MSM	All ranks
Mentioned In Dispatches, MID*	All ranks
Citation for Gallantry Award*	All ranks

* Not strictly a medal.

By 1911, 79% of the population lived in towns (2). At the beginning of the twentieth century: 20% lived in poverty; 15% at subsistence level and 10% below subsistence level. The main cause of poverty was low wages, and the main cause of extreme poverty was the loss of the main bread winner. Government was beginning to address this poverty but in modern terms was only just scratching the surface. 1909 brought in the first old age pensions at 5s (25p today) a week and was for the over 70's only, and in 1911 sickness benefits for workers were introduced.

In 1914 the average working family lived in two up two down houses and the very poor often in just a single room. The following is an account of such housing (3).

The types of housing varied widely, but the poorest houses would be built of mud and cement with a thatched roof. In Godshill one such dwelling had a small sitting room, a wash house downstairs and two bedrooms upstairs. Rather better houses were built of brick and slate and had two rooms on two floors. The estate houses were largely of brick and tile and could be up to three bedrooms with two reception rooms. The poorer housing has probably been pulled down (1).

Some houses in Strelley that were demolished in the 1960s only had access to the upper floor by ladder.

In the 1911 census the number of rooms in a property was recorded. These could include a kitchen but not a scullery, landing, lobby, closet or bathroom. This

7

gives the opportunity of seeing the sort of living conditions of the families of the men in the villages in 1911: number of rooms and the size of the family (see Appendix 4).

Some 60% of the family income was spent on food. In 1900 the working week was 54 hours which left little time (and money) for leisure. In fact leisure, except for alcohol, was non-existent for one third of the working class (3).

General life expectancy in 1914 was 50 for men and 54 for women (in 1918 the conscription age was raised to 51!). In 1901 the upper-class could expect to live for 60 years which was double that of the very poor and in 1901 those aged 60-64 accounted for only 2.7% of the population. A positive for the residents of Bilborough and Strelley was that life expectancy was higher in the countryside than in the towns (1).

The main occupations of the men of Strelley and Bilborough were agriculture, mining and as domestic servants. In 1911 the Edge family at Strelley Hall employed ten servants (mostly women) within the Hall itself. Working hours were long and leisure time short for the working man and woman. At the turn of the century many workers received a half day on Saturday, working until 12-00. Others were not so fortunate and agricultural workers could work a full seven days a week, depending on the season. Shop workers worked 80-90 hour weeks and domestic servants even longer. For more detail on hours of work and wages see Appendix 5.

During the war years the government introduced rent controls and housing costs were pegged to those of August 1914 levels (3). In addition to poor housing and food, in 1914-1918 education was elementary, and health care almost non-existent for the poor. On the introduction of conscription in 1915, 80% of recruits were found to have such bad teeth that they could not eat properly and less than 30% had a satisfactory standard of health and strength (1). Very many were rejected as unfit on account of those defective teeth, in fact 70% of British recruits were considered to be in need of dental treatment. The forces recognised that the general bad state of teeth was a threat to the health of the troops and introduced dentists into the army (5). Many of the recruits could be treated to a standard that would meet military requirements. Early in the war, to this end, the dental profession offered its services for free to those potential recruits that required such treatment.

THE BRITISH ARMY

The British Army in 1914 required a recruit to be 5 feet 8 inches tall and between 18-35 years of age. He could not be sent abroad until he was 19 although during WW1 many were, including some from Strelley and Bilborough.

The recruit could join the Regular Army and after service the Army Reserve and then be called up if needed. At the start of the war it numbered 733,514 men (4) see Table 3.

From all combatants, 70 million men were under arms in WW1 of whom ~9 million (13%) died. Death from disease accounted for ~1/3 of the deaths. In the British Army a total of 908,371 were killed, 2,090,212 wounded and 191,652 held prisoner giving a total of 35.8% casualties.

In 1914 the 733,514 men of the British Army was small in number when compared to the conscript armies of Germany, France and Russia. During the war a further 4 million were recruited from England and a total of almost 5 million from the UK as a whole. Over 700,000
(excluding Empire troops) were killed (c. 14%) and c. 2.3 million were wounded of whom 64% returned to front line fighting, 18% to garrison duty and sedentary occupations, 8% were invalided out and 7% died of wounds (4) see Appendix 7

TABLE 3. BRITISH ARMY RECRUITMENT FIGURES
British army recruited from within the British Isles

Standing army as of August 1914	733,514
Recruited thereafter	
England	4,006,158
Scotland	557,618
Wales	272,924
Ireland	134,202
Total	**5,704,416**
With Empire and Dominion troops	**8,689,467**

The numbers vary from one source to another depending on precise definitions, the difficulties in making accurate recordings at the time, and the loss and later destruction of records. In Strelley and Bilborough, of those listed in the Roll of Honour, 10% were killed with a further man dying of illness without leaving England and fighting: if he is included the total rises to 12.5%. Two further men, who were invalided out of the army, died very shortly after the war bringing the total to 17.5%. In the Roll of Honour book 11 of the 40 were wounded (27.5%) which includes the two who would die almost immediately after the war. The military records were found for a further 30 men, who lived in the village in 1911, and who would have been of military age between 1914-1918, in addition to the forty in the Roll of Honour book. One of these men was killed in the war. If these men are included then 7.14% died. The men who were wounded or who discharged due to sickness in the total number of 70, numbered 29 (41.4%) (Appendix 7).

Between the declaration of war against Germany in 1914 to January 1915 over one million men had volunteered to enlist (7), helped by the famous Kitchener poster, with the slogan "your country needs you". However the recruitment was not sufficient to keep pace with casualties. The government saw no way other than to introduce conscription, compulsory enlistment, to keep pace with the need for men in the armed forces.

In March 1916 the 'Military Services Act' was passed which imposed conscription on all single men between the ages of 18 and 41. The Act was not popular and over 200,000 protested against it in Trafalgar Square in April 1916. A second Act, passed in May 1916, extended conscription to married men as well. In the first year many men failed to respond to the call up but despite that 1.1 million were enlisted.

When conscription started in 1916 it was possible to be exempted by appealing to their 'Military Service Tribunal'. If exempted they were said to be starred. By June 1916, 748,587 men had appealed (6a).

Many of those appealing were given an exemption of some duration ranging from a few weeks to six months. Permanent exemption was conditional upon their circumstances not changing. By October 1916 the number of exempted men, or men who had cases pending, numbered 1.12 million. By May 1917 the number had risen to 1.8 million, a number which exceeded the number of troops serving overseas (6b). Those exempt from service needed to be in occupations that were vital to the war effort and which could not be done by others. Some of the reserve occupations were (8):

Driving trams/buses
Mining
Shipyards
Munition factories
Farms
Clerics
Police officers
Medical professions
Teachers
Where a family business could be damaged
Food production, butchers and bakers
Conscientious objectors

The main occupations of the villages, mining and farming are listed. It could be expected that quite a number of men may have been able to claim exemption. Indeed the entry for Joseph Woodhouse in the Roll of Honour book, refers to him as a Regimental Quartermaster Sergeant mobilised August 4th, 1915 and being released from military service in June 1916 for food production.

The Daily Telegraph reported a number of sample cases. One which would have been of interest to Bilborough and Strelley men, was one brought by a 'Tobacco and cigarette' manufacturer (a major tobacco company, probably John Player, which had a factory in Nottingham) on behalf of one of its blenders. The plea made was that the company 'supplied army officers' but it was rejected (9).

Some 5.5 million men were of military age in 1914, a figure supplemented by 500,000 who reached the age of 18 each year. It is estimated that 2.5 million men were in reserve occupations in 1918. 4.9 million men were enlisted between 1914 and 1918. 2.4 million enlisted before conscription and 2.5 million after it, of which 1.3 million were actually conscripted. It is estimated that less than 35% were forced to serve. Recruits were classified into four classes of fitness A, B, C and D ranging from fit, A, downwards, Appendix 8: in 1918 75% were classified as A.

Of the men who volunteered nationally, 40% were rejected for medical reasons. This was because of malnutrition which was widespread. The height of a 15 year old working class boy was 160 cm (5' 3") and one from the upper class was 171 cm. (5' 7"), (10).

The images of the Great War usually bring to mind the fighting on the Western Front in France and Flanders. It was of course a world war and men served in a number of theatres of war: the main ones can be found in Table 4.

TABLE 4. WHERE THE BRITISH ARMY SERVED

	Peak No.	In Total	Died
France and Flanders	2,046,901	5,399,563	564,715
Mesopotamia	447,531	889,702	
Egypt and Palestine	432,857	1,192,511	
Salonika	285,021	404,207	
Italy	132,667	145,764	
Gallipoli	127,737	468,987	26,213
Other	293,096	475,210	
On all other fronts			365,375
Total			**956,703**
Wounded			**2,272,998**

The places served by the men listed in the Roll of Honour book, can be found in Appendix 9.

Strelley had a male population of 97 and Bilborough 106. There were 135 men of military age, including those who moved in after 1911 as determined by those recorded in the Roll of Honour book, or would be, over the course of the war. The military records of 70 are known or probably known. The remaining 55 may not have volunteered or not been conscripted for reasons outlined earlier, or their records were lost or destroyed.

The regiments joined by the men of the villages can be found as Table 5.

Five men were killed out of the 70 known to have served, 7%: this compares with 10.2% for the British Empire. 14 were wounded, 19.7% compared to 23.5% for the British Empire. A further 10 men were found to have been treated for sickness which included such debilitating diseases as malaria. Full details can be found in Appendix 7.

There were 21 men between the ages of 36 to 44 in 1911. These would have been available for conscription by 1915 (aged 18-41) or in 1918 when the age limit was raised to 51. Family records indicate that the curate of Bilborough, St. Martin's church, enlisted in 1914: no army position was given but it could be assumed it was as a chaplain. A further 19 were schoolboys in 1911 (ages 10-13) and of these records were found for 11 (57.9%). Records were found for 58 of the remaining 96 men (60.4%)

In 1918, in all, nationally, some 2.5 million men were enlisted. After the 'Military Services Act' it is not possible to know whether a man would have volunteered or was conscripted when he reached the age of 18. Those much older than the minimum age of conscription we can safely assume were conscripted, since they would have volunteered earlier if that had been their intention.

TABLE 5. REGIMENTS JOINED
Roll of Honour book 40

Sherwood Foresters	10
Artillery	10
Royal Army Service Corps	4
South Notts. Hussars	3
RFC/RAF	4 (1 also included as Artillery)
Royal Navy	2
Coldstream Guards	2
Lincolnshire Regiment	1
London Scottish Regiment	1
Royal Engineers	1
Royal Marines	1
Royal Ordnance Corps	1
Royal Army Medical Corps	1

Others

Sherwood Foresters	12
Artillery	4
Royal Army Service Corps	4
RAF	1
Royal Engineers	2
Labour Corps	1

Of these 64 men the popular choices were:

Sherwood Foresters	22
Artillery	14
Service Corps	8

Many military records were destroyed after the Great War and it is possible that some of the men who apparently did not enlist, had done so but their records were destroyed. Others were probably in the exempt categories (see earlier). The only obviously handicapped men were John Henry Beardsley who is described as deaf in the handicap section of the 1911 census and James Henry Flack who had been paralysed from birth.

It is worth repeating here that the general health of the population in the early part of the 20th Century was much lower than that of today, with the poverty enforcing a poor diet and living conditions, with basic or no medical care. In 1917-1918 only 36% of the conscripts were passed as fully fit for service. The army grades of fitness levels, Appendix 8, and those known for the village recruits, where recorded, can be found in Appendix 10.

At the start of the war the country had an all volunteer army and the height requirement was 5' 8". This was soon dropped to 5' 3" presumably because most men were only at that height (see earlier). Until the spring of 1916, all men were volunteers. The reasons men chose to volunteer will be as varied as the number of men themselves. However there will be some factors which will run as a thread through their decision making.

We probably think first that they were patriotism, glory and the attraction of the uniform: I'm sure a uniform would be seen as making them a 'babe magnet' then as now: although they would probably have phrased it differently.

However there may have been other more prosaic reasons. Employment that involved long hours, was hard and poorly paid, may have been a driver towards volunteering. In both villages coal mining, agriculture and domestic service were the main occupations.

Housing was probably poor and much of it tied cottages. Large families were squashed into small houses. Most of these young men had probably never had a bed of their own, let alone a room. The army would have offered them their own bed if not their own room. The 1911 census included as part of its returns the number of rooms in a house, as well as the occupants. The living conditions of each of the men can thus be assessed. Conditions relevant to a particular man are included in the profile of each – see later.

Food would have been difficult to come by: a family then would have spent c. 40% of its income on food compared to less than 10% today. The army, on the other hand, provided a diet of over 3000 calories per day. Similarly clothes would have been few, whereas the army would have provided several full changes of clothing including that all important uniform.

Recruits would have the chance for foreign travel and since the early volunteers believed it would be all over by Christmas, they could be there and back having had an adventure. After the war some of the returning men said they had enjoyed the experience. "Many young men enjoyed the guaranteed pay, the intense comradeship, the responsibility and much greater sexual freedom than in peacetime Britain" (11). Additionally "Many soldiers enjoyed WW1. If they were lucky they would avoid a big offensive and much of the time the conditions might be better than at home" (11).

Positive feelings about the war can easily be felt after the war was over, when a man was grateful for surviving, or at the beginning of a war before the realities of it became clear. When it became clear at home what was happening on the Western Front and Gallipoli, the rate of volunteering dried up somewhat. Poor wages and hard work were probably preferable to death or injury. It is likely that some men on reaching the military age would have volunteered although probably in fewer numbers than before. The introduction of conscription was as a counter to the too few volunteering. Some women gave men who had not enlisted a white feather. Men who had joined, but had been discharged from the army, were awarded the 'Silver War Badge'. This was worn on the lapel of civilian clothes to signify that they had served to avoid them receiving that white feather. Individual profiles of the men recognise those from the villages who received the 'Silver War Badge'

It is also interesting to note that of those from the villages of Bilborough and Strelley who joined after 1916, fewer joined the infantry than the earlier volunteers. In part, this may have been an assumption that it was better not to be in the front line and 'going over the top'. It is also likely that the first volunteers were those men who were fit and in good health. Later conscription took in all men for evaluation regardless of health and fitness. Many would have been unfit and rejected and those sufficiently healthy, if not completely so, were inducted but put to serve in less arduous tasks such as garrison duty (see Appendix 8).

These aspects of life are developed in greater detail in later chapters.

Living conditions in Strelley and Bilborough

Would the living conditions experienced by the population of the two villages have influenced whether a man joined up or not? In the first years it would have been to volunteer or not, and in the later years whether to be conscripted or try to gain exemption. The main occupations of agriculture and mining were both on the list of exempt occupations.

The working class population at the beginning of the 20th century lived in two up two down (four roomed accommodation). The 1911 census recorded the number of rooms in each household. For the purpose of working out whether the male population shared bedrooms it was assumed that a four roomed dwelling had two bedrooms and that a three roomed dwelling also used two of its rooms as bedrooms. Larger houses, five rooms could be three up two down, four up one down. Married couples were assumed to have a bedroom of their own, although in some of the really crowded houses this might not have been the case. The remaining bedrooms would be divided between the sexes both children, lodgers and visitors. In some of the smaller houses with large families it was possible that the sexes shared a bedroom with a curtain dividing the room. In large families it was likely that a number of brothers shared the same bed, with parents probably "topping and tailing" them. It is not possible from the census returns to determine the size of the rooms and therefore the likelihood of getting more than one bed into the room. On the whole it could be assumed that dwellings would be smaller rather than larger for working class people.

From the 1911 census are found 135 males who were or would be of military age during 1914-18. It is estimated that 67 (50%) probably did not share a bedroom with 58 (43%) sharing: 2 men were already in the forces and were in barracks and 8 were not found.

Taking those aged 9 up to and including 11, 32 (80%) were likely to share at least a bedroom, 5 (13%) unlikely and 3 could not be established.

The age group 17-25 inclusive had 17 (41%) likely to share and 19 (46%) not with 5 not found. See Table 6 for a more complete picture.

Of the age group most likely to volunteer, 14-25, only one was married. Discounting this man, 30 (57%) were likely to have shared a bedroom and 23 not. When taking the group in the Roll of Honour book the figures are 13 (62%) and 8. Of the 40, four volunteered as officers, an indication of them coming from a wealthier background. These four lived in bigger houses: three of them were from the Edge family that lived in the Hall. If the four are subtracted from those not sharing a room, the figure for those that do rises to 76%.

The occupations of the 135 men can be found in Table 7. Most of the men worked either in agriculture, the mines or domestic service. The percentages for the various groups are: 69 for all the men; 64 for those for whom military records are known and 55 for those in the Roll of Honour book. Setting aside those who were still at school in 1911 the remaining men would probably have been in higher paid jobs, even if marginally so. The distribution of the occupations amongst the most popular regiments can be found in Table 8.

TABLE 6. LIVING CONDITIONS OF THE MEN OF BOTH VILLAGES

Age group	Number in group	Probably sharing a room			Married
		Yes	No	Unknown	
0-13	21	18	3	0	0
14-18	26	16	7	3	0
19-25	34	14	17	3	1
26-34	30	6	23	1	18
35-44	24	4	20	0	22
Total	135	58	70	7	41

Roll of Honour book					
0-13	11	9	2	0	0
14-18	11	9	2	0	0
19-25	13	4	6	3	0
26-34	5	0	4	1	4
Total	40	22	14	4	4

The five categories in the tables account for 42/70, 60% and 26/40, 65% for all men enlisted and those in the Roll of Honour book respectively.

Most of those in agriculture and mining found their way into the infantry (Sherwood Foresters), servants into the artillery and apprentices, although small in number, into the RFC/RAF.

The Sherwood Foresters attracted 10 of the 40 men listed in the Roll of Honour book: 50% were from agriculture and 30% from mining. When of age, those of school age in 1911, none chose the Sherwood Foresters. Was this because by the time of conscription the population had become aware of the slaughter on the Western Front, and with that knowledge, they chose some other theatre of war or a position behind the lines? With food shortages, as a result of the German blockade, what had been a struggle previously to find enough to eat became even more difficult, with a corresponding drop in fitness as a result. This could have resulted in the number of B and C classifications increasing, resulting in fewer potential recruits being seen as front line fighting men.

It is difficult to assess servants versus self employed: gardeners have been assumed to work for a particular family with one assessed as self employed.

WORKING HOURS AND PAY

At the turn of the century many workers received a half day on Saturday working until 12-00. Others were not so fortunate and agricultural workers could work a full seven days a week depending on the season. Shop workers worked 80-90 hour weeks and domestic servants even longer (3).

The pay scales for the military are listed in Appendix 11 and those for various trades in civilian life in Appendix 5.

Different sources give a different average wage in 1914. Two of these give the following. For a basic 58 hour week: 16s 9d which had risen to 30s 6d for a 52 hour week in 1918 (12). A second, determined the average wage in 1913-1914 to be 26s 8d per week or £69 p.a. (3).

For the two of the three main occupations of the two villages the following would have been the likely rate of pay in 1914. For miners: the average wage for a miner in South Wales was 9s per day; (x 5.5 days = £2 9s 6d per week) (13). Miners however worked mostly on piecework and from their pay would be deducted, the costs of equipment and time lost for illness or injury.

An agricultural labourer would expect to earn a wage of 16s 9d for a 58 hour week (13)

Compare these to the pay of a private or equivalent in the army:

-infantry   1s 1d per day
-artillery   1s 2½d per day
-RASC   1s 2d per day

Table 7. Occupations

Occupations	All No.	%	Served No.	%	Roll of Honour book No	%
Agriculture	44	32.6	20	28.6	11	27.5
Mining	34	25.2	15	21.4	7	17.5
Servants	15	11.1	10	14.3	4	10
School	12	8.9	5	7.1	5	12.5
Apprentices	4	3	3	4.3	3	7.5
Factory workers	3	2.2	2	2.9	1	2.5
Blacksmiths	2	1.5	1	1.4		
Clerks	2	1.5	1	1.4	1	2.5
Council workers	2	1.5				
Insurance agents	2	1.5	2	2.9	1	2.5
Brewer	1	74				
Clerk in holy orders	1	74	1	1.4		
Commercial traveller	1	74				
Fitter	1	74	1	1.4		
Gardener	1	74	1	1.4	1	2.5
Merchant	1	74	1	1.4	1	2.5
Own means	1	74	1	1.4	1	2.5
Publican	1	74				
Railway worker	1	74	1	1.4		
Teacher	1	74	1	1.4	1	2.5
Traction engine driver	1	74				
Woodman	1	74	1	1.4	1	2.5
Unknown	3	2.2	3	4.3	2	5
Total	**135**		**70**		**40**	

Table 8. Occupations by Regiment

All men

Regiment	Agriculture	Mining	Servant	Apprentice	School
Sherwood Foresters	9	9		1	
Artillery	5	1	4	2	
RASC	2	2			
RFC/RAF	1	2	1		
S. Notts. Hussars	2			1	

Roll of Honour book

Regiment	Agriculture	Mining	Servant	Apprentice	School
Sherwood Foresters	5	3	1		
Artillery	2	1	4	2	
RASC	1	1			
RFC/RAF			2	1	
S. Notts. Hussars	2			1	

Knowle Park Farm, Swingate
Cutting corn during the Great War
using a McCormac binder and a Fordson tractor.
In the photo left to right are:
J W Blant, gamekeeper, gamekeeper, Tommy
Kettle (lived in Beg House, a police house in
Swingate).
One keeper was from Nuthall and the other Strelley
Hall, probably Harry Herbert Underwood.

Photograph courtesy of Mr John Blant

Fig. 6 Corn cutting in Strelley during the Great War

Great War Harvest Scene
Using a McCormac Deering Binder
and a Fordson Tractor Model N?
Photograph courtesy of Mr John Blant

Fig. 7 Harvest scene in Strelley during the Great War

18

The poorest paid private in the army could earn c. 45% of an agricultural worker's pay. The agricultural worker would need c. 40% of his pay to provide food whereas for the recruit all was found. The recruit would have more than adequate food and clothing whereas the poorest labourers would struggle to provide themselves with an adequate diet. A sergeant in any of the above branches of the armed forces could exceed the average wage in 1914. It was unlikely that a recruit in the villages would have assumed they would make sergeant, although some did. However the living conditions within the army would have appeared quite attractive to many. Set against this would be the discipline of the army compared to the relative freedom of civilian life and in a war the possibility of being killed or wounded. Each man would have seen things from their own perspective of crowded living, poor diet and healthcare or if fortunate enough a comfortable living.

The following are the profiles of all of the men who went to war from the villages. Their war record is detailed and any photographs included. Their occupations, size of family and living conditions are described. Hopefully this will put a name to a statistic and a face to a name. Maps of the parishes showing the houses will give some idea of where they lived and who were their neighbours. Some photographs of their houses as they were then, and as they are now if earlier photographs are not available, are included to further round out the picture. Some images of the farming life of the period have also been included.

INDIVIDUALS AND THEIR FAMILIES

Table 9 shows the numbers given to the houses in the villages by the enumerator on the census returns of 1911. The start of the census, **1**, was at St. Martin's House on the border of the parishes of Bilborough and Strelley, but in Bilborough. It was the house of the curate of the Bilborough parish church of St. Martin of Tours. The census finished at the house of John Ryder, **89**, in Strelley.

Maps have been constructed of both parishes from those of the Ordnance Survey of 1914 and 1915. The map of the complete parish of Strelley can be found as Fig. 8 and the relatively heavily populated area of Main Street as an enlarged map, Fig. 9. A map, Fig. 10, of Bilborough parish is rather large and contained what is now part of Broxtowe and Cinderhill. The village centre can be found on an enlarged map, Fig. 11.

The route of the enumerator around the two villages was followed by using the known names of houses and their enumerator number, where recorded, and then positioning those unknown in between. Sometimes the name of the road is given. These are sometimes given on the Ordnance survey maps and are used if not known already, with others deduced from current names and local knowledge. The census numbers are marked on the maps where the houses are known, giving the reader the opportunity to see exactly where the men of the village lived in 1911 and by extension probably did so between 1914 and 1918.

There would of course have been movement in and out of the villages in that time. However these maps will give some idea of whether the men lived in isolated positions or in the centre of the villages and who their neighbours were.

The enlarged maps of the main areas of the two villages have been constructed because of the relatively large number of dwellings in a small area that would otherwise make the print difficult to read on a large map.

TABLE 9. 1911 CENSUS NUMBERS AND NAMES

Bilborough			Strelley		
No.	Surname	Address	No.	Surname	Address
1	Thomson	St. Martin's House	46	Sly	Strelley Lane
2	Papworth		47	Simpkin	Strelley Lane
3	Pinchin		48	Wheatley	Strelley Lane
4	Faulconbridge T		49	Stevenson	
5	Mellor	School House	50	Phillip	Catstone Farm
6	Wilson			Oaglen	Catstone Farm
7	Breedon		51	Dunmore	Old Rectory Farm
8	Chambers		52	Burton	Old Rectory Farm
9	Goode		53	Edge	Strelley Hall
10	Sibey			Dawn	Strelley Hall
11	Allen	The Elms	54	Wright	Dairy Cottage
12	Hardy	The Rectory		Wilson	Dairy Cottage
13	Fletcher		55	Hill	
14	Carlyle		56	Blatherwick	Old Moor Farm
	Wilkinson		57	Paling	Strelley Fields
15	Brewster		58	Monks	Turkey Field Farm
16	Murden		59	Housley	Spring Wood
17	Pike		60	Morley	Strelley Park Farm
18	Burton		61	Whitney	Swingate Farm
19	Booth		62	Stevenson	Gate House
20	Musgrove	Old Manor House	63	Raynor	Bridle Road
21	Eley	Old Manor House	64	Parkins	Bridle Road
22 ``	Wagstaff	Old Manor House	65	Stevenson	Boggart House
23	Booth				Springwood Side
24	Flack		66	Bradshaw	
	Raynor		67	Henson	Mill Farm

20

TABLE 9. CONTINUED

Bilborough			Strelley		
No.	Surname	Address	No.	Surname	Address
25	Murden		68	Green	Top Lodge
26	Woodhouse		69	Headland	Hall Farm Cottage
27	Stevenson Dean		70	Powell	Hall Farm
				Wallbank	Hall Farm
28	Woodhouse			Samways	Hall Farm
29	Frain W	Saddle Room	71	Porter	Hall Farm
30	Stevenson	Machine Houses	72	Heron	
31	Taylor	Machine Houses	73	Barnes	Gardener's Cottage
32	Tuckwood		74	Underwood	The Kennels
33	Andrew	Broxtowe Hall	75	Oldershaw	
	Baines	Broxtowe Hall	76	Smith	
34	Cordon	Cinderhill	77	Charlton	
35	Richards	Cinderhill	78	Cooper	
36	Henson	Cinderhill	79	Payne	Broad Oak Inn
37	Moore	Chilwell Dam House	80	Massey	
38	Moore	Chilwell Dam Farm	81	Smith	
39	Jackson	Bilborough Lane	82	Cooper	
40	Hipwell	Bilborough Lane	83	Dunmore	
41	Boyfield	Bilborough Lane	84	Beardsley	
42	Frain T	Bilborough Lane	85	Davenport	
43	Greenham	North Lodge	86	Margetts	
44	Woodhouse Burton		87	Faulconbridge	Post Office
			88	Faulconbridge	
45	Pursglove		89	Ryder	Park Hill Cottage

REFERENCES: FIGURE 8 Appendix 13 Page 113
FIGURE 9 Page 22
FIGURE 10 Appendix 14 Page 114
FIGURE 11 Page 23

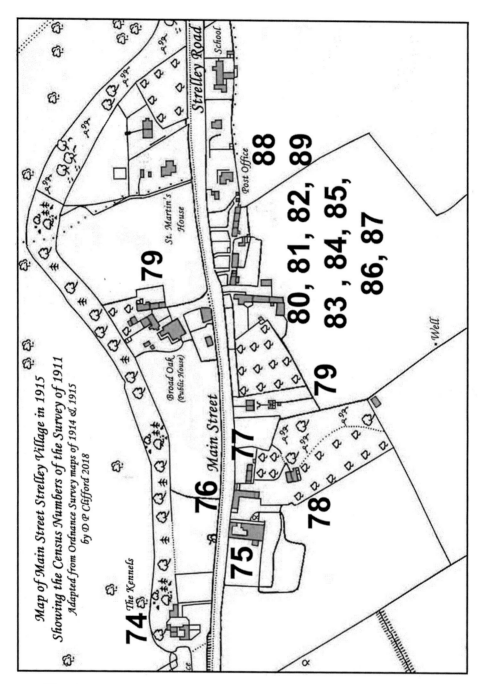

Fig. 9 Enlarged map of Main Street, Strelley village, showing the
census numbers in 1911

22

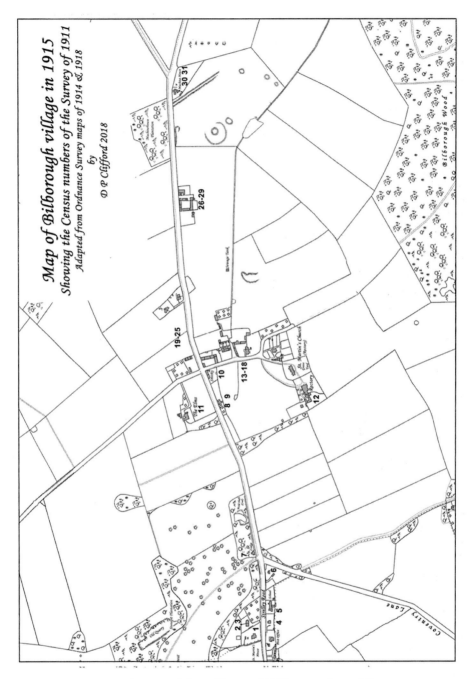

Fig. 11 Enlarged map of the village of Bilborough and the census numbers of 1911

23

FAMILIES

There were 203 males in the villages of whom 117 were of military age, or would become so over the period to 1918. At least 18 others came into the villages after 1911. The Roll of Honour book lists 40 men of whom only 22 were in the villages in 1911. It is not clear how the Roll of Honour book was compiled and where the records contained in it came from. Clearly the records of those killed must have come from family, friends and possibly the authorities. Some of the remaining 95 men would have moved away and others not joined or were maybe exempt for one reason or another. The military records of a further 30 men were found. Of the remaining 65 men some of the records may have been lost or destroyed, but for many it was not possible to narrow down a large number of candidates to a particular person in the villages' census of 1911. The list of men, the results of searches, or reasons for the absence of data, can be found in Appendix 12.

The records show, probably quite logically, that a higher percentage of the younger men in 1914 served compared to those who were older.

Those age 12-25 in 1914	53 went (65%) and 28 did not (35%)
Those 26 and greater	18 went (33%) and 36 did not (67%)
Those up to 30 in 1914	62 went (60%) and 42 did not (40%)
Those 31 upwards	9 went (29%) and 22 did not (71%)

Particular families had a large number of men who were, or who would become, of military age. The Hensons had 6; Goodes, 5; Booth, 4; Burton, 4; Flack, 4; Moore, 4; Smith, 4; Stevenson, 4; Brewster, 3; Dunmore, 3; Edge, 3; Faulconbridge, 3; Green, 3; Hudson, 3; Jackson, 3; Woodhouse, 3.

Five of the six who died during the war came from these families: Brewster, Flack, Goode, Green and Henson with a Hudson dying immediately after the war. A member of the Palin family was the fifth who was killed in the war. There were two men who came to the villages, probably after their military service, and died immediately after the war; Hughes and Pauley.

Those who gave their lives during the war are written about first. They are followed by those who died during or immediately after the war and who have military headstones in Strelley churchyard. Other men who served are then described in the sequence that the census returns were made in 1911. Finally, those who did not die and were not resident in the village in 1911 are listed and follow the census numbers in alphabetical order.

The family name and the names of the men who served are marked in bold.

THE MEN WHO DIED WHILST ON ACTIVE SERVICE AND THEIR FAMILIES

15. Brewster family

John Thomas Brewster (1865 00 00), from Rutland married Rowetta (Rose) Davey (1864 00 00), from Somerset, in 1894 and moved to Bilborough where their eldest child George E. was born. In the 1901 census they were living in Strelley with four more children, Edith G, 4; William John, 3; Wilfred Charles, 2 and Selina 8 months. From the 1911 census a further child (Clifford) Thomas (1903 00 00) had been born, John had died and Rose as she was now listed moved back to Bilborough. It is likely that she was living in extreme poverty, see earlier statistics (2), and 'conditions of life in 1914'. She earned a living as a charwoman and lived in a tied cottage with a half yearly rent of £3 payable at Lady Day and Michaelmas: in 1911 she received a rebate of 16s.

The census describes her children as: **George**, 15, a domestic gardener, born in Bilborough; Edith, 14, a domestic servant; **William**, 13, a domestic odd job boy; **Wilfred**, 12; Lena, 10; and Thomas, 8, and all born in Strelley.

A letter to the local paper told how during WW1 she lived in St. Martin's Cottages opposite the church of that name, and was the post mistress. She then lost George, killed in the war, one of her daughters who died after a bicycle accident in the nearby Aspley Lane, Thomas who was killed in a pit accident and Wilfred who got married but died young of cancer five years later. The letter also indicates that at least some of the Brewsters worked for the Edge family. Records show that Edith died 1927 03 00, (Clifford) Thomas died 1937 09 00 and Wilfred Charles 1940 00 00, in Liverpool, having married Gertrude G Greaves in 1929. Rose herself died in 1958 aged 95.

In 1911 the family lived in 6 rooms. Assuming this was a two down four up Rose could have had a bedroom of her own with the two girls sharing a further room and 2 boys each in the remaining rooms. If only three of the rooms were bedrooms then it is likely that the four boys shared a bedroom and possibly a bed.

The two oldest boys joined up very early in the war. **George** was first, joining up barely a month after war had been declared. His brother **William John** joined up at 17 and was serving in France by August 1915: this was probably illegal since recruits had to be 19 to be sent abroad.

15. George (Edwin George in the Roll of Honour book) **Brewster** joined the Royal Field Artillery, 251 Battalion, Northumbrian Brigade, on Sept. 16th, 1914, aged 19, as a gunner. He must have been one of the first of the early volunteers. He was in action at Ypres (1915), Somme (1916) and Arras (1917). He was taken prisoner on April 27th, 1918 and died at Dercy behind the German lines on Sept. 20th, 1918. He had survived almost the entire war before being captured and dying as a prisoner, less than two months before Armistice Day. Little is known about him, including his war service, probably because he wasn't able to give a first hand account to the compiler of the Roll of Honour book, and it is probable that his family only knew the barest of details of his service. He is buried in the churchyard at Crecy sur Serre and his name is inscribed on the war memorial in Strelley churchyard see Fig. 12.

15. William John, also joined the Royal Field Artillery on Dec. 15th, 1914 aged 17. Records describe him as a miner and his service number as 1020754R. He served in France from August 8th, 1914 to October 5th, 1918. This meant that he was sent to fight in France whilst still short of his eighteenth birthday: the British Army rules stated that a person could join the forces at 18 but could not be sent abroad until they were 19! He fought at Hooge, Dec. 25th, 1915 and at Ypres, Somme and Arras before being demobilised on Dec. 15th, 1920. After the war he probably married Alice M Smith and moved to Nottingham where he is recorded as a Potato and Fish Fryer Shop keeper in the 1939 Register. He died in 1959 aged 61.

15. Wilfred Charles also joined the Royal Garrison Artillery as a signaller on April 2nd, 1918 when he was 19. His records describe him as a collier aged 19 years and 122 days with a fitness of Category A and a service number 206781. He served at Crome (did this mean Cromer) and was demobilised on Dec. 4th, 1918. The electoral roll of 1928 found him living at The Mount in Bilborough with his mother Rose and his brothers William John and Clifford Thomas. He probably married Gertrude G Greaves in 1929. He is not found in the 1939 Register: this is strange since a record of the death of a Wilfred John Brewster was found, 1940. All of Rose Brewster's sons served in the army, Royal Garrison Artillery, but for Clifford Thomas who was too young, being only 15 in 1918.

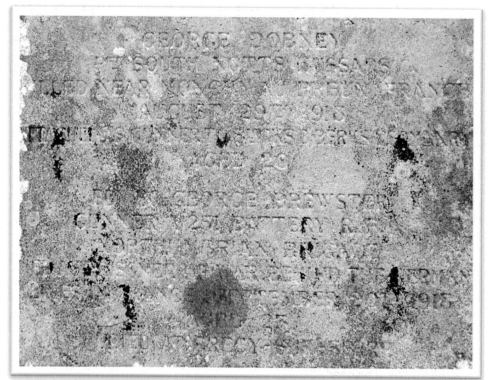

Fig. 12 War Memorial inscription to George Brewster and George Dobney

43. George Dobney (1897 00 00). He is included here because he shares the same plaque on the war memorial as George Brewster. In 1911 he was living with his parents in Gosberton in Lincolnshire and came to the village after the Census. No record could be found as to where he was living in the village. In 1911 he was living with his parents George, 47, a farm labourer and Jane 43. They had been married 26 years and had had 14 children of whom 12 were living. Eight, four boys, aged 3, 6, 13 and 20 and four girls, a baby, 7, 11, 15 were living at home with their parents. In addition there were three male boarders. George was then 13 years old and still at school. The house had eight rooms and despite the size there would have been extensive bedroom sharing. George almost certainly would have become a farm worker of some sort in such a rural area where agricultural jobs would be the norm. That asks the question as to how he came to have moved to Strelley by 1914? The answer can be found in the history of another army recruit from the village, George Greenham (**43**). In the 1911 census his wife is listed as Ann, 22, who it turns out was Ann Dobney who married George in 1910. In the 1911 Census she is recorded as being from Crowland, Lincolnshire (the older Dobney children listed in the 1911 census were born in Crowland). Additionally the 1901 census lists her. It is likely that she travelled to become a servant at one of the big houses, possibly, the Hall. George may then have joined her in the village between 1911 and 1915. Since it is not clear where he lived his address here has been assumed to be that of his sister.

He enlisted on Oct. 7th, 1915, aged 17 and presumably almost 18. He joined the South Notts. Hussars, service numbers 2187 and 281976 and later the Berks. and Bucks. battalion of the Machine Gun Corps service number 165606. **Sidney Scott Henson** (**67**) was already in the South Notts. Hussars and the two served in the same theatres of war from that point until George's death. They may have been friends in peacetime. They would have lived quite a way apart; the Greenhams lived on the immediate edge of Bilborough village and the Hensons on the furthest side of the parish of Strelley. It is of course possible that George boarded with the Hensons.

He served in Egypt and Palestine from June 1917 to May 1918. He was present at the taking of Beersheba and in the pursuit of the Turks after the fall of El Nuggar during which his horse was killed under him. He embarked for France on the S S Leasowe Castle on May 26th, 1918 (as did Sydney Scott Henson) which was torpedoed on May 27th. He re-embarked on June 17th, and trained in France as a machine gunner. He joined the reserve line as a gunner on Aug. 25th, 1918 and was killed near Monchy au Preux, Arras on Aug. 29th, 1918. He is commemorated on the war memorial in Strelley Churchyard, Fig. 12, and on the Vis-en-Artois Memorial in France.

The Nottingham Evening Post of May 30th, 1918, reported the British naval loss of a transport, torpedoed in the Mediterranean with the loss of 101 lives. It was the Leasowe Castle. The dead included 13 military officers and 79 men.

The ship's company lost the captain, two wireless operators and 6 ratings. The article then describes the Leasowe Castle as a steel, twin-screw steamer of 9737 tons gross register, built in 1915, by Cammel, Laird and Co., Birkenhead, for the Union Castle Mail Steamship Company. She was 488ft. long, and had a 58ft. beam.

A letter to the Post on May 16th, 1919 pointed out that "midnight 26-27th May is approaching. Cannot a memorial service be held for the gallant local lads who faced death so nobly on the ill-fated troopship Leasowe Castle. It will be remembered that it fell to the lot of the South Notts. Hussars to do the submarine guard after the troopship had been torpedoed – hence the heavy toll on the regiment. The discipline and bravery was truly great." On May 21st the Post reported "A service to the memory of the South Notts. Hussars who lost their lives by the sinking of the Leasowe Castle, in the Mediterranean, will be held on the first anniversary of the event, next Tuesday evening, in St. Mary's Church, Nottingham."

Whether Sydney Scott Henson and George Dobney were part of that submarine guard will never be known.

24. The **Flack** family lived in Bilborough in 1911. It was headed by **Terrell**, who was 43 and a gamekeeper, with his wife Martha Maria, 49. He was born at Lakenheath in Suffolk and she at Weeting in Norfolk which is near Thetford and not far from Lakenheath. They had six children, all living, of whom four were living with them in Bilborough: three sons and one daughter. The house in Bilborough had 5 rooms: notionally 3 bedrooms. One bedroom was presumably taken by the parents, a second by their sister and therefore leaving the three boys to share the third. The two younger boys were born in Weeting, Norfolk and the older in Hatchern, London whilst the youngest child, the girl, was born at Blidworth Vale in Nottinghamshire.

The oldest son, 22 in 1911, James Henry, does not appear in the Roll of Honour book. This is not surprising since he is described in the 1911 census as paralysed from birth. However a James Henry Flack, described as being born in 1888 in Greenwich, London to Turrell and Martha Maria Malt, is recorded as marrying Margaret E Warnes in King's Lynn in 1944.

24. George Terrell Flack (1892 00 00), was born at Weeting, Norfolk. In 1911 he was 19 and made a living as a tobacco blender. He volunteered on Sept. 2nd, 1914 for the Royal Medical Corps. as a private: service number 31231. He served in France from May 1915 to October 1917. He served on His Majesty's Ambulance Transport "Brighton" from March 1918 to March 1919. During 1915 and 1916 he was involved in various engagements in the Ypres sector with the 14th division at Vimy Ridge and at the Battle of the Somme. On June 7th, 1917 he was involved with the capture of the Messines Ridge with the 25th division. He was wounded at Vimy Ridge May 16th, 1916. He was demobilised on May 3rd, 1919.

After the war he probably married Dorothy S Veal in 1923 in Downham (Market). The 1939 Register describes him as widowed and working as a foreman on a BAT stemming machine at the Player's factory and living in Nottingham. He died, 1958 01 24, in Nottinghamshire.

24. William Richard Flack (1895 00 00), his brother, was working as a milk delivery boy in 1911. He volunteered as a driver in the Royal Field Artillery on Sept. 2nd, 1914 (the same date as his brother George), at the age of 18 with the service number 99607. He served in Egypt and Gallipoli where he was killed on Dec. 2nd, 1915, aged 19. He is buried at Anafarta Sagir Suvla (Suvla Bay) and buried on Hill 10 Cemetery: grave ref. II.A.3.: Commonwealth Grave Number 607119. He is commemorated on the War memorial in Strelley Churchyard, Fig. 13.

57. Alfred Palin married Eliza Ann Wilkinson, 1880 12 18, at All Saints, Strelley. By 1891 they had four children and he made his living as a miner. By 1901 two of the children had left home and **Alfred John Palin** (1895 00 00) had been born, with the family living at Robinette Collapse on the border of the parishes of Strelley and Cossall. 1911 found them in a six roomed house, with Alfred John, now 16, working as a coal ganger. Alfred John shared the house with his parents; sister, Mary Ann, 21; a nephew, 5; and a visiting aunt, 61, who worked as a 'useful ladies maid'.

The Roll of Honour book entry is very sparse considering he joined early in the war. This may be due to the family only having the briefest of details about him and he not being there to add more. The book records him as joining the Royal Field Artillery in Dec. 1914, as a Bombadier. He served in France from Aug. 1915 to May 3rd, 1916. He was killed on May 3rd, 1916 and is buried in the French Military Cemetery, at Ecoivres, Mont-St. Eloi, NW Arras. He was 22. His grave reference is I.A. 26 and it has a Commonwealth Grave Number 65901. He is also commemorated on the Calvary War Memorial in Strelley Churchyard, Fig. 13.

Fig. 13 War memorial inscription to William Flack and Alfred Palin

29

68. In 1911 the **Green** family lived at Top Lodge in Strelley having been at Alfreton in the 1901 census. Sam, 45, was a farm labourer and he and his wife of 18 years, Eliza Ann, 48, had eight children, all living. The eight were resident with them in Strelley, with six of them boys, 18, 16, 14, 10, 7 and 1 and two girls, 12 and 5. The oldest three were born at Riddings in Derbyshire, the next two at Eltham in Kent and the youngest three at Mansfield, Beeston and Strelley respectively. Their house had 5 rooms with three, notionally bedrooms. It was likely that the boys had to share a bedroom and probably a bed. As a family they had clearly moved to Strelley between 1906 and 1911. Three of the Green boys were eligible for military service but none appear in the Roll of Honour book and it is very likely that the family moved on yet again before 1914, possibly to Warsop or thereabouts.

68. Charles Walter Green (1894 09 00) was described in the 1911 census as a stock boy, underground. C W Green born at Riddings enlisted in the Sherwood Foresters 2/8th battalion at Warsop (just north of Mansfield) as a private, army number 306726: this was probably Charles Walter Green. He was killed in action in France and Flanders,1917 04 07, at Le Verguier, Aisne, Picardie in France. He is buried in the Commonwealth War Cemetery at Vadencourt, Maissemy which is near St. Quentin.

68. The military record of his older brother **Fred Green** (1892 00 00) was more difficult to find. In the 1911 census he was working as a miner, underground, as a pony driver. A Fred Green enlisted in the Sherwood Foresters and served 1914-1920 as a private, army number, 106776.

Towards the end of the war, in spring, 1918, he married Ada A Osborne in Nottingham. He left London for Sydney in 1921 on the 'Bendigo' and arrived in Australia, 1922 01 02. The reasons for his emigration are not clear nor what he did until his death at Helensburgh, NSW, 1925 07 27. There was an inquest on the 27th of July.

68. Very little was found about a further brother, **George Edward**, (1896 07 17) who in 1911 also worked as a miner, pony driver, underground. No military record was found that fitted his details. A George is found in the 1939 Register working as a miner in Warsop and married to an Edith A. He died 1989 05 00 with his death being registered in Newark.

THE MEN WHO DIED AS A RESULT OF THE WAR, AND THEIR FAMILIES.

67. There were two **Henson** families (**36 and 67**) in the villages. The Henson family that lost a son was headed by Thomas, 53, formerly a miner but in 1911 a farmer, and his wife Mary Ann, 48. They had been married 26 years and had six children: five of them were living at home, all of them sons. Their ages ranged from 14-25 and they would all therefore have been of military age during 1914-1918. They lived at Mill Farm which had six rooms and there would therefore have been some bedroom sharing.

67. Charles Wilfred Henson (1892 00 00) enlisted on June 20th, 1918, as a private in the Sherwood Foresters, service number, 119042. It is not clear why he enlisted at such a late date. A Charles W Henson married Annie Jukes in 1916. He was trained at Salt Fleet and Ipswich but died of Cerebral Meningitis in Ipswich Military Hospital on Aug. 20th, 1918. He is buried in the churchyard at Strelley, and on his military headstone is inscribed, "Blessed are the pure in heart for they shall see God", see Fig. 14. He has been given a Commonwealth Grave Number, 2749862.

67. Thomas Cecil (1886 02 05) a miner, was the oldest. He is not recorded in the Roll of Honour book and no military record from any other source was found. Electoral rolls of 1921 and 1922 show him to be living at Mill Farm and therefore was still local. This and his absence from the Roll of Honour book are a strong indication that he either did not enlist or was rejected by the military forces. It could have been that as the oldest son he was required to help his aging father run the farm and on these grounds granted exemption. He married Mary E Johnson in 1912. The 1939 Register records him as a dairy farmer at Park Farm, Strelley with his wife Mary E.

Fig. 14 Military headstone of Charles W Henson

Harold Henson, brother of Charles Wilfred and Sydney Scott Henson (Both Roll of Honour), at Turkey Field farm in the 1920s.

Photograph kindly supplied by Mr John Blant

Fig. 15 Harold Henson

67. Harold Henson (1887 09 04) was also a miner in 1911. Like his brother Thomas Cecil he is not recorded in the Roll of Honour book and no military record could be located elsewhere. He married Sabina Johnson in 1914 and the two of them are recorded in the electoral rolls of 1921 and 1922 living at Turkey Field Farm, Strelley, Fig. 15. The 1939 Register records him as living at Swingate Farm with Sabina and possibly two daughters. He died in 1970, aged 83.

67. Samuel Renny Henson (1889 10 04) was also a miner in 1911 and went on to be a farmer. Like his brothers he remained in the village and is recorded on the electoral rolls of 1921 and 1922. No military record could be found for him. He married Fanny Stevenson in 1915. The 1939 Register has him farming Rectory Farm with Fanny and helped by his son Arthur.

67. Sidney Scott Henson (1896 09 27) the youngest of the sons was the first to enlist in Dec.14th, 1914, aged 18. He joined the Yeomanry, South Notts. Hussars and served in Salonika from Dec.10th, 1916 to Aug. 1917; Egypt and Palestine Aug. 1917; and France June 1918 to Feb. 1919 when he was demobilised on the 3rd of that month. No mention is made of the period of enlistment to the end of 1916 although he may have been stationed in England since service abroad was, officially, not allowed until a person reached the age of 19. He was stationed at Rafa and took part in operations to take Beersheba and Jerusalem. He then embarked on the Leasowe Castle which was torpedoed off Alexandria the same night. He re-embarked on June 17th for France where he trained as a machine gunner. He was in action at the storming of the St. Quentin Canal at Bellenglise and took part in several minor engagements. He served throughout the latter part of the war with George Dobney (**43**) until the death of his friend.

After the war he married Sarah E Everett in 1924. In the 1939 Register he was living at Church Farm Cottage with Sarah, working as a poultry farmer and assisting his brothers, Fig. 16. He died in 1942, his death being recorded in the Long Eaton Office. Local knowledge has it that he was knocked down and killed on a foggy November day, by an American military lorry, near Moorgreen. It seems ironic that he survived the entire First World War only to be killed in a domestic road accident in the second.

The Roll of Honour book lists three **Hudsons**. Thomas, a shepherd, and Jane Hudson had four sons and a daughter according to the 1901 census and were living in Brackley. **George** 15 and **William** 14, were both agricultural labourers. Their brothers, **Robert Atkinson**, 12, and **Edmund**, 5, were still at school. The three older brothers were born at Lonsladdale in Westmorland with Edmund being born at Doncaster in Yorkshire. By the time of the 1911 census the brothers had dispersed with Robert Atkinson in Chesterfield and Edmund in St. Neots. It was not possible to locate William.

The 1911 Bilborough/Strelley census lists no Hudsons. Thomas and Jane moved at some point to Home Farm in Strelley and it is likely that three of their sons had joined them there. George clearly did not come to the area, or did not serve, since he is not listed in the Roll of Honour book.

Edmund Hudson (1894 00 00) lived in 1911 at a boarding house run by Alice Willoughby at Shaftesbury Avenue, St. Neots. There were four male boarders ranging in age from 16-61 with Edmund the youngest. Also in the house was the landlady's daughter who was 9. Three of the boarders, including Edmund, worked for the Great North Railway (GNR) as clerks. In 1915 he was living with his parents Thomas and Jane as recorded on his discharge papers.

He joined the London Regiment (London Scottish) as a private, service number 5724, on Nov. 24th, 1915, aged 18. His enlistment medical report shows him to have been 5' 7.5" tall, weighing 9st.12lb and with a chest measurement of 38".

He trained initially on home duties until sent to France 1916 04 06. He was in action at Vimy Ridge and in the Battle of the Somme on July 1st, 1916 where he was wounded. He spent time in hospitals at Etaples. He was returned home to hospital in Glasgow where he was treated for shell shock over a period of 22 days. His brother Robert Atkinson talked of surviving the war untouched but the same could not be said for Edmund. He was returned to hospital with acute bronchitis and released after 20 days. He was discharged from the army on Nov. 24th, 1917 according to the Roll of Honour book but his discharge papers show he was discharged Nov. 25th, 1916 in consequence of para 392 XVI King's Regulations (no longer physically fit for war service). His military character was good and his character was described thus "This man has a good character and is steady and well conducted. He served in France for 3 months."

Sydney Scott Henson (Roll of Honour) walking towards the Motte from Strelley church in 1927

Photograph: Nottingham Guardian

Fig. 16 Sydney Scott Henson

He is described as 22, 5' 8" with a chest measurement of 38" with an expansion of 3". He had brown eyes and dark brown hair and was described as a clerk by trade. His home address was Home Farm, Strelley. After discharge he returned home to live there with his parents and was awarded a pension of 20s per week. He died 1919 11 24 at the age of 25 and is buried in Strelley church graveyard, Fig. 17. The grave has a Commonwealth Grave Number, 2749863.

William Hudson was the oldest of the three and the one of whom the least was found. The Roll of Honour book records that he joined the Lincolnshire Regiment April, 1917, aged 30, and trained at Grimsby. He served in France from Oct. 1917 to Dec. 21st, 1918. He was stationed at Merveille and was in action on Lys Front and Nieppe Forest in March, 1918. He was wounded in the abdomen and spent time in hospital at Airs in France and Colchester and Norwich. He was discharged 1919 04 19. The name Hudson was quite common and a first name of William even more so. Many records, during and after the war were found, but none could be tied with any degree of certainty to William.

His brother **Robert Atkinson Hudson** (1889 00 00), on the other hand, had fairly unique first names. The 1911 census found him at Manor Cottages, Scarcliffe, near Chesterfiield. He was a horseman on a farm and boarded with William and Eleanor Lancaster and their four young children, two boys and two girls. William and Eleanor were from Westmorland and may have been family friends or relatives. The house had five rooms and Robert may have had to share a bedroom with the two boys.

Fig. 17 Military headstone Edmund Hudson

He volunteered very early and joined the Sherwood Foresters on Sept. 7th, 1914: his service number was 16982. He served in France from Sept. 1st, 1915 to Mar. 6th, 1919. He was in action at Loos, 1915; Ypres, Messines Ridge, Vimy Ridge, and the Somme in 1916 and Ypres, 1917. He was involved in the advance on the Cambrai Front up to the time of the Armistice and was demobilised March 1919. The book records that he was never wounded or had a day's illness during the time of active service. Nothing was found about him after the war and he does not appear in the 1939 Register.

The Hughes family was not in the local census of 1911.

54. Harry Alfred Hughes (1879 00 00) was recorded in the 1891 census as being born to William Hughes, 53, a tailor, in Wolverhampton. At the time William was a widower and Harry was earning a living as a journeyman wheelwright. He must have moved to one of the villages after that, since his military record is in the Roll of Honour book.
He joined the Royal Army Ordinance Corps as a private on Nov. 2nd, 1916, service number O/24687. He served at Aldershot and then in Mesopotamia, stationed at Margil (Basra) and Baghdad, from July 1917 to July 1918. From July 1918 to May 1919 he was on garrison duty at Muttra and Meerut in India. During that time he was in hospital at Diolalie and Bareilley. He was demobilised on May 25th, 1919 and discharged 1919 06 22.
An army pension document describes him as enlisting 1915 12 07 as a private in the Royal Army Ordnance Corps regimental number 024687. He was evaluated for deafness in the right ear, 1916 08 29, with a grade/category of Bl.
In 1918 09 00 he had his right testis removed, the cause of which was described as by active service conditions and his disability put at 70%. In 1919 09 00 he had the removal of a secondary growth. He was given a grade IV discharge 1919 06 22. The document was dated 1920 02 05 and written across the document is the word, deceased. Whether he received a pension is not clear but beneath the description of his operation are the words 'claim under act.' He died one year exactly after his discharge and four months after the pension review document. His death was clearly due to testicular cancer.
After the war, and before his death, he lived with his wife, Margaret, at Dairy Cottage, Strelley village and died 1920 06 22, aged 41. He is remembered with a military headstone in the graveyard of All Saints church, Strelley, Fig. 18. After the description of his military service the inscription says "peace perfect peace".

Pauley Edward (1879 00 00) was born in Stamford, Lincolnshire and married Susannah Francis at St. Martin's church, Stamford, during the third quarter of 1902. In 1911 he was living at 10 Malting Yard, Water Street, Stamford, with his wife and five children, three girls (aged 8, 7, 3) and two boys (5, 9½) and was a labourer. A form awarding him a Silver War Badge, dated 1917 06 11, details his enlistment as a sapper in the Royal Engineers as

1916 11 15, number 241893. He was discharged from the 1st. Prov. Co. on 1917 06 15 with the cause given as 392, xvi, sickness. He did not serve overseas, and his badge number was 198121.

He died in Strelley 1920 03 09, aged 40, the husband of Susan Pauley of 8 Babbington, Strelley. He is not recorded in the Roll of Honour book. He has a military headstone in All Saints Churchyard, Strelley. The family inscription reads "ever in our thoughts", Fig. 19.

Fig. 18 Military Headstone Harry A Hughes

Fig. 19 Military Headstone Edward Pauley

Those living in the village that served and survived

They are numbered according to that given to their family/house, by the enumerator, during the 1911 census. These numbers can be found on the maps of the villages and their parishes - see earlier.

1. Ernest Montague Thomson (1870 07 08) was a curate at St. Martin of Tours church in Bilborough in 1911. It was initially assumed that as a clergyman he was automatically excluded from war service. However, in following his life, a family tree submission was found, that refers to his military service. No details were given and it has been assumed here that it was as a chaplain. He was born in London and married Louisa Dawson, 1901 07 09. At the time of the 1911 census he was living on Main Street at St. Martin's House, the house for the curate of the parish of St Martin, with Louisa and their son Jamie aged five.

He was the Rector of Bladon and Woodstock church, 1929-1936 and in 1939 was living at Lymington in Hampshire. He died at Kessingland in Suffolk, 1960 02 05 aged 89.

As a clergyman he would have moved from church to church, and may well have moved on from Bilborough before joining up as a chaplain. As a result he would not be found in the Roll of Honour book.

2. The Pinchin family lived in a four roomed house in Bilborough in 1911. **Edward Pinchin**, 43, was born in Gloucestershire and had married Louisa Clarke, from Herefordshire, in 1895 at Worcester. They had three children all of whom were living. In 1911 Edward was working as a farm labourer and Louisa as a domestic laundress. The house was rented from the Estate at £2 10s per half year, and the Estate Rent register showed that he was still resident at Michaelmas, 1918. In addition they had a boarder, Ellen Gould, 21, who was a Laundry Maid.

Edward would have been too old for conscription in 1916 but would have just been within the extended age, of 51, in 1918. Since he was resident in the village for the whole of the war, and is not recorded in the Roll of Honour book, it is very likely that he was not conscripted. Additionally, searches for a military record yielded nothing. The Pinchin family probably lived in the cottage on the left of the photograph, Fig. 20. He died in 1958, aged 91, in Nottingham.

His three children consisted of **James Edward Pinchin** (1896 05 13), born at Upper Warley in Worcestershire, and his two younger sisters. In 1911 James was 14 years old, and described as a fitter's apprentice. In 1916 he would have been 19 and eligible for conscription. He was not conscripted until 1918 when he would have been 21. It is possible that his conscription was deferred to allow him to complete his apprenticeship. The Roll of Honour book describes him as joining the Royal Air Force on April 11th, 1918. He is described as a Corporal, but that is probably a later promotion. His service number was 160119. He trained in the Flying Sheds at Terhill Aerodrome in Shropshire: this description would indicate he was a member of a ground crew and the RAF was using his apprenticeship engineering skills. After training he was utilised on Home Service and was demobilised April 1919.

Further research confirms most of the above but adds that his occupation was as a fitter and erector which would indicate that he had finished his apprenticeship. He died 1974 10 06 in Nottingham.

There were two members of the **Faulconbridge** family available for military service (entries **4 & 88**).

4. Thomas Faulconbridge, (1874 00 00). In 1911 he lived with his wife of 11 years and their three small children, in a five roomed house which was rented from the Estate at £2 10s per half year. He was a stationary engine driver at a colliery, the younger brother of James' father Joseph, and was born in Strelley. He is not included in the Roll of Honour book and no clear military record was found for him. At the introduction of conscription in 1916 he would have been 41 and unlikely to have been called up. He would have been eligible at the age of 43, in 1918, when the age limit was raised to 51. His name is found on electoral rolls after the war, and, whether called up or not, he survived the war. He probably lived at the house in Fig. 21.

Fig. 20 Houses numbered 2 & 3 in the 1911 Census

5. William Street Mellor (1881 02 16) was born to William, a Blacksmith, and Eliza in Ilkeston. He was still living with his parents and his four brothers in 1901 and earning a living as an Elementary School Teacher, as was one of his brothers. He married, 1908 09 05, Ellen Roberts in Ilkeston. At some time after 1901 he moved to teach in the village school in Bilborough. The 1911 census records him as living in the School House, Fig. 23, with Ellen, 27, also an elementary school teacher, and their daughter, 1. He can be seen in a wedding photograph of James Faulconbridge wearing his sailor's uniform.

His entry in the Roll of Honour book is quite detailed and long. He is described as the Headmaster of Bilborough & Strelley School: no other entry records the occupation of the person. He was a Petty Officer First Class in the Royal Naval Volunteer Reserve. His service number was Z/5174.

40

He joined on June 18th, 1916 and trained at Crystal Palace. He transferred to The Royal Navy Jan. 19th, 1917 and was attached to the Merchant Fleet Auxiliary. He was in the War area from Jan. 17th until the Armistice, on HMS Satellite and MFA No. 455. He was engaged on Special Service taking loans in kind, such as coal, to the Allies, chiefly to Genoa, Naples, and Leghorn and bringing back iron ore from Algiers and other ports. He also went to Cuba for sugar and New York for flour, where news of the Armistice was received.

His ship sank a German submarine off the coast of Algiers on Oct. 26th, 1917. The ship was chased by a submarine on the last voyage between Finisterre and Lisbon. It was also severely damaged in a collision off Cape St. Vincent, with only twelve ships out of a convoy of thirty reaching Gibraltar. He was discharged May 6th, 1919.

The only reference found for him, after the war, was the 1939 Register when he was living in Worksop, with his wife Ellen, and earning a living, as before, as an Elementary School Teacher.

Fig. 21 House numbered 4 in the 1911 Census

41

Fig. 22 William Mellor in uniform

6. James William Wilson (1893 08 19) was living with his father George, 46, a woodman, and his mother, 44, Elizabeth (nee Padget), his younger brother, 7, and sister, 4, in 4 rooms in Bilborough in 1911. The house is probably number 6 on the 1911 Bilborough census route and is now known as Woodman's Cottage. His parents were from Lincolnshire but their children were born elsewhere with James at Brough, and his brother and sister at Danethorpe. He was 17 and a farm labourer. In the 1901 census George was a shepherd on a farm, and visiting them were two young sisters from Bradford, Florence and Lilian Padget.

The family must have emigrated to the United States of America some time after this. He next appears on a US WW1 draft registration card which gives the following details.

He was 23, born 1893 08 19, at Brough, Newark, England, and living at 21 Soledad Street, Santa Barbara, California. He was a janitor at St. Joseph's Home in Stockton City. He was described as Caucasian and single, an alien, but also that he had served six months, as a private, in the infantry in England. He is described as short, medium build with grey eyes and brown hair, but not balding. It was also established that he was not disabled. The document is dated June 5th, 1917.

The next military record is his Attestation Paper on joining the British Army. It describes him as born in Brough, aged 23 and 11 months and dated 1917 08 09. His address was given as 21 Soledad Street, Santa Barbara, California and his occupation as a locomotive foreman. He joined the Royal Engineers, Inland Water

Transport Battalion, service number RE320652. A further source has him joining the Royal Engineers, Inland Water and Dock Companies, service number 341917, and his father named as George.

A further record is a United States WW2 draft card of 1942. On that he is living at 372 N. Fair Oaks Avenue in Pasadena. He is 49, born 1893 08 19, has no phone and was born in Nottingham. The person who will always know his address is Elizabeth Wilson living at E. Montceito Street, Santa Barbara, California. His employer was a J. Adams, 2005, Arcadia Avenue, E. Arcadia, California.

It is intriguing to know that prior to June 1917 he had served six months in the infantry in England. This seems a very short period to have signed up for even in peacetime. Although, had he fled to the USA to escape the war, it is most unlikely that he would have returned to England and risked punishment by the army. More likely is that he emigrated with his family to the USA with permission of the military? When the USA entered the war and were about to draft him he returned to Britain and joined the British Army. On the face of it, it was Home Service but it could have included time abroad. He obviously returned to the USA and received his draft card for WW2 there.

It is also interesting that to the US authorities in June, he describes himself as a janitor and in August in England as a locomotive fireman. It unlikely that they are two different people since on both occasions the same address was given.

A family tree contribution has him living in Santa Barbara, 1938; in 1940 04 01 with his mother and in 1942 when he was described as divorced.

Fig. 23 School and School House numbered 5 in the 1911 Census
43

9. Goode family

John Goode aged 46 in 1911 was born in Ruddington, Nottinghamshire, and married Fanny Parker, from Sproxton, Leicestershire, in Nottingham, 1888 12 05. Fanny died in 1907 and John then married Ann Maria Goodhead from Carlton, Notts.. John and Fanny appear to have had six children 5 boys and a girl, Mary, the youngest. Mary does not appear in the 1911 census. In 1911 the boys were **Thomas W.**, 1889 07 17, 21, born in Ruddington , **John**, 1893 07 14, 17, **William**, 1894 09 15, 15, both born in Bunny, Notts., and Harry, 1900 01 08, 11, born in Bilborough. The other son, Alvin, (1892 11 11) 18, born in Bunny, was a servant with a family in Clifton. The Goode household also included John's step-daughter Jennie Edie Thomson who was 15 and born at Hyson Green, Nottingham.

The house had 5 rooms for 7 people 5 male and 2 female. Assuming the house had three bedrooms then it is likely that John and his wife had one, Jennie had one and the four brothers shared the other. It is possible that Alvin went out as a servant to ease the accommodation pressure in the house.

Thomas W was a cowman on a farm; John was a 'trammer' in the mine; William an assistant domestic groom with Harry still at school.

Thomas, Alvin, John and William all served. A search for records for Harry gave 48 options but insufficient data was available to narrow the options down to just Harry. Thomas, Alvin and William can be found in the Roll of Honour book but not John. It is likely that John moved out of the family home and was living in an adjacent parish and thus not recorded in the Roll of Honour book. It may be that Alvin returned home from Clifton and was living in Bilborough when he enlisted or used his parents address on enlistment, and was thus included in the book.

9. Thomas Goode

(1889 07 17) enlisted in the Sherwood Foresters as a private Dec. 11th, 1911. He was therefore a serving soldier when the war began. He married Florence Howe in Nottingham in 1912. His service was in France from Nov. 6th, 1914 to Aug. 27th, 1918. He was at Neuvechapelle, Mar. 10th, 1915; Somme, Sept. 25th, 1916; Lens, July 1st, 1917 and Cambrai, Nov. 19th, 1917. He was wounded in his arm, shoulder and side on Mar. 10th, 1915 at Neuvechapelle, in the hand at the battle of the Somme and suffered a slight wound to the neck at Lens. He was seriously wounded on Aug. 14th, 1918 and was discharged from the army Feb. 2nd, 1919.

The Nottingham Evening Post reported on May 26th, 1915, that Private T Goode, of the 1st Sherwood Foresters, of Bilborough, Strelley, was wounded March 12th and was now in hospital at Llandudno. This must have been his wound at Neuvechapelle and must have been serious enough for him to require recuperation at Llandudno. The photograph shown is presented, Fig. 24. He spent 2 years in India. The Roll of Honour book does not record this and he may have been stationed in India prior to the start of the war. The Post also reported on July 7th, 1917 under the heading "Local casualties, Wounded, Sherwood Foresters" one Goode 11733 T (Bilborough). This must have been his neck wound suffered at Lens.

After the war the electoral roll of 1925 showed he and Florence were living in the Trent ward in Nottingham. The electoral roll of 1929 found him living at Moores farm, Bilborough without Florence, but with his brothers John and William. The 1939 Register places him living with his father John Goode, his brother William and a Jane (b. 1893 02 03). Thomas is described as a farm labourer and William as a general labourer. They lived at St. Martin's Road Cottages, Fig. 25, the same address as Rose Brewster and her family. There is no clear evidence of the date of his death.

Fig. 24 Thomas Goode in dress uniform

9. Alvin Goode (1892 11 11). According to the 1911 census, he was living at Clifton and working as a farm servant. The house was that of a farmer John Butler and his wife Emma both aged 68. Their son and daughter in law with their baby son shared the house. Additionally there were four teenage servants, two female and two male of which Alvin was one. The house had ten rooms. A minimum of four bedrooms would be required: a room for each couple (assume the baby is with the parents), one for the girls and one for the boys.

The Roll of Honour book lists only his name, regiment (Sherwood Foresters) and rank (private). Other sources show that he enlisted 1915 12 12, aged 23 and 1 month, and given the army number, 89284. He is described as a coal miner living with his father John in Bilborough.

After the war he married Gladys E Burnden in 1920 when he was 29. The 1939 census described him as a colliery hewer living with his wife Gladys in Nottingham. He died in March, 1940 in Nottingham.

9. In 1911 **William Goode** (1894 09 15) was 16, living with his family in Bilborough and earning a living as an assistant domestic groom.

He enlisted in the Royal Field Artillery as a driver, on May 7th, 1915 when he was 20 years and 7 months old. His army number was L25293. He served in France from Jan. 11th, 1916 to Jan. 6th, 1919. He was in action on the Somme, July 1st, 1916; Arras, April 6th, 1917 and Paschendale, Oct. 17th, 1917. He was in the retreats from Cambrai, Mar. 21st, 1918 and Armentieres, April 9th, 1918 and the advance from Ypres Oct. 19th, 1918. He was discharged from the army Jan. 6th, 1919.

It is probable that he never married and little can be found about him after the war. The 1939 Register has him living with his father John at St. Martin's Road Cottages. He is described as single and a general labourer.

Fig. 25 St. Martin's Cottages probably in the block 13-17 in the 1911 Census

9. John Goode (1893 07 14) does not appear in the Roll of Honour book. In 1911 he lived with his family in Bilborough and earned his living as a "trammer" in the mines. He had clearly moved out of the family home after 1911 and his attestation paper records him living at 15 Charles St., Hucknall, but still making his living as a miner. He joined the Sherwood Foresters on June 1st, 1915 when he was 19 years and 350 days old and was given the service number, 26755. He was promoted at some point to lance corporal and was discharged with class P wounds May 5th, 1917 and given the Silver War Badge on 29th Aug., 1917.

Little can be found about him after the war. He is included on the electoral roll of 1927 with his brother Thomas, and in 1929 living at Moores farm with his brothers William and Thomas. He also appears in the 1939 Register. He was living at 49 Savile Road, Southwell and was still a miner but now described as an "onsetter" (a miner who loaded tubs into the cage at the bottom of a mine shaft). He lived in Southwell with his wife, Nellie (Mary Ellen) and two other people of whom only Janet Haycock (Goode), (1935 07 12), is named, who could well be his daughter. He died at Bilsthorpe, 1957 01 09, aged 63.

Bilborough had two Sibey brothers living in the village in 1911.

10. George Henry Sibey (1879 03 12) was the oldest, a general village blacksmith from Barsingham, Lincolnshire. He had married Edith Annie Oxspring, in Chapeltown, Yorkshire, 1906 06 21. His local address is not known but may have been at the top of St. Martin's Road, Fig. 26. The house had five rooms and living with them was George's brother, Sydney, and Harry Smith who was a general blacksmith's apprentice from Basford. There are no military records that can be clearly attributed to him.

A George Sibey had joined the Sherwood Foresters, 7th Reserve Battalion, service number, 305162, in 1912 04 11. He was awarded the Silver War Badge, number 128007, which was issued, 1917 10 08. His service number was 305162 and it records that he enlisted 1912 04 11 and was discharged 1917 09 13. He may have joined as a "weekend soldier", since as a recently married man, in a respectable trade; it is unlikely that he would have signed up as a regular full time soldier. He does not have an entry in the Roll of Honour book and may have left the village.

The 1939 Register has him living at Skipton in Yorkshire with his wife Edith A, and earning a living as a shoeing and general smith in agricultural engineering.

10. Sydney Sibey, (1888 03 23), George's brother, lived with him. He was born in Stapleford, Lincolnshire, was single in 1911, and a blacksmith at the colliery. He married Bertha Victoria Charlton in Strelley in 1912 09 12.

He enlisted 1915 01 02, at Nottingham, in the Royal Army Service Corps, 185th/159th Company, regimental number TS5190. He is described as a shoeing smith married to Bertha and having one child, Marjorie, 1914 02 28, and living at 17 Beresford Street, Radford, Nottingham. The enlistment officer sent a request to the manager of Wollaton Collieries for a character reference for Sidney Sibey. He was described as 5' 8" tall with grey eyes and black hair. He had worked at the colliery for 4 years and 9 months. He was described as a shoeing smith and satisfactory. The reply was dated 1915 01 05.

On a form describing his character for the purpose of being sent home for discharge he is described as being with the 60th Field Ambulance. He had only been with them for six weeks but in that time was described as sober (as far as they knew). To their question "is he reliable?" the entry was, 'fairly but not specially

47

so'. He was described as intelligent and as regards aptitude in civilian life he was described as a fairly good farrier. The document was dated 1917 02 19. His enlistment form described him as 26 years and 9 months, 5' 8" tall, chest 35" and plus 2" expanded. As a distinguishing mark he had a scar on the front of his left thigh.

The 1939 Register has him living with Bertha at 73 Hardy St., Basford and earning a living as a colliery blacksmith. He died Dec. 1939, aged 51.

Fig. 26 Probably the old Smithy numbered 10 in the 1911 Census

10. Harry Smith (1894 00 00). In 1911 he was living with the George Henry Sibey **(10)** and was working as a blacksmith's apprentice originating from Basford. No definitive records for him could be determined from the 3463 found.

14. Frederick Carlisle, (1897 00 00), is listed in the Roll of Honour book as serving with the Royal Flying Corps. It is not clear why no record is included.

The 1911 census has him living with his widowed mother Sarah and his sister, Nellie, 23, in Bilborough. He was 14 years old and an apprentice engineer. The 1901 census describes Sarah as a widow and living in Church Road, Bilborough with three of her children, all born in Bilborough, one of whom was Frederich, aged 4. Sarah had been married to Frederich, a miner who died, 1895 11 03, aged 39. Frederich was baptised, 1896 09 02, at St. Martin of Tours, Bilborough with his father named as Frederick, a miner, and Sarah his mother with his own name spelt Frederick. The census was conducted on April 2nd, 1911 which would make his birth after that date if he was born in 1896, since his age is given as 14.

Searches for his military record found one that included his mother's name, Sarah Carlyle, and his address Church ? (unclear), Bilborough. He is described as 5' 2.7" with a chest of 34" and by trade a fitter. An F C Carliell was in the Royal Flying Corps., as an Air Mechanic 1st Class with a trade as tinsmith and sheet metal worker. His service number was 46127 and he transferred to the Royal Air Force in 1918. A further source described him as F C Carliell, in the Royal Air Force in 1918, with a service number of 46127 and also with his trade as a tinsmith and sheet metal worker. His Air Force pay was 4s 0d. This was from 1916 05 29 with a seniority date of 1917 04 01. In 1916 he would have been 19 or 20 and may have joined after completing his apprenticeship.

The **Burton** family had three members who would have been of military age during 1914-1918. None of them appear in the Roll of Honour book. Whether they did not serve or moved to another area was very difficult to determine. No military records were found that could be specifically attributed to them, primarily because their names were so common.

18. John Henry Burton, 29, was the oldest, married, and a farmer according to the 1911 census. Ninety possible records were found in the search for any military details for him. The Estate Rent register showed that he rented two properties at Michaelmas 1914: one with a half yearly rent of £117 10s and the other £2 10s: so obviously a wealthy man. He is recorded in the Estate Rent book in 1918, which showed he was still in the village, had probably gained exemption and survived the war. A John Henry Burton died in Redhill in 1955, and if this was him, it would confirm his survival.

18. John Burton, his brother, (the Burtons seemed to lack imagination with first names), 20, was single and described as an apprentice engineer. The search for a military history turned up even more records, 377, than for his brother, probably because a refining term such as 'Henry' was not available.

For the youngest **William** see entry **44**.

Two families named Booth lived in, Bilborough in 1911.

19. William Edward Rogers Booth (1881 07 25). He was born in Radford to William Edward, a Blacksmith in Radford, and Mary (nee Rogers). He was baptised at St. Leonards Church, Wollaton and married Margaret Macae in the first quarter of 1910.

In 1911 he was living at the Old Manor House in Bilborough with Margaret and their infant son Ronald Howard and making his living as a Blacksmith. The house had five rooms.

Searches for a war record failed to turn up an accurate fit to him. He may of course have been still in the village and not conscripted or failed on some grounds to be accepted. He may have moved to a nearby parish and so did not appear in the Roll of Honour book.

The 1939 Register has him and Margaret living at 22, Bridge St., Nottingham, with their daughter Joan. He was working as a colliery blacksmith. He died, 1945 02 07, in Nottingham.

The second family consisted of the parents John Henry, 48, a blacksmith and Laura his wife, 48: and their 10 children all of whom were living. Nine of the children were living with them; four daughters 9, 18, 24 and 25 and five sons 6, 11, 13, 15, and 29, in a 5 roomed house which must have been very crowded.

23.   John Henry Booth (1897 10 29) is the only one to have been included in the Roll of Honour book. In 1911 he worked on a farm.

He joined as a private in the Royal Field Artillery on Dec. 12th, 1914 when he was only just over 17. He transferred to the Royal Flying Corps on Mar. 14th, 1915 and served in France as a Sergeant in the 25th squadron stationed at Auchelle from Jun. 2nd, 1916 to May 22nd, 1917, service number 4790. During that time he was involved in bringing down seven German machines:

-a Fokker on July 3rd, 1916 that crashed at Don.
-a Focker on Sept. 7th, 1916 that crashed at Loos.
-a Fokker on Sept. 7th, 1916 at Lens.
-an Albatross on Jan. 23rd, 1917 that was driven down at Henin-Lietard.
-a Halberstadt on Jan. 29th, 1917 that was driven down at Douai.
-an unknown hostile machine on Mar.17th, 1917 that crashed at Pont-a-Voudon.
-an Albatross Scout on April 18th, 1917 that crashed at Don.

He was an observer, but if he had been a pilot he would have been described as an ace for bringing down seven aircraft.

He was awarded the Italian Bronze Medal for Military Valour, May 22nd, 1917. "His Majesty the King of Italy has awarded the Bronze Medal for Military Valour. His Majesty the King has given unrestricted permission in all cases to wear the decorations and Medals in Question".

He then trained in England for a commission and was gazetted as a second Lieutenant, Sept. 23rd, 1917 and then as a Flying Officer Lieutenant, April 1st, 1918. He was noted as Lieutenant (Observer) in the 1918 R.A.F. list (the RAF came into being on April 1st, 1918) and was demobilised on Feb. 18th, 1920.

He probably married Ethel Pinchin in 1929 (she was the sister of James Edward Pinchin of Bilborough). He was not found on the 1939 Register, but someone of the name died in 1983 09 00 aged 85 in Nottingham.

Fig. 27   Farm house probaby in the block 13-17 in the 1911 Census

Two other Booths also served but must have moved out of the villages before the war.

23.   Joseph William Booth (1895 04 11), John Henry's brother, who was described as a Tobacco Machinist in the 1911 census. A family tree posting describes his marriage to Sarah Ann Grainger, at Aldecar, 1911 04 15: he would have been 16. He was not entered into the Roll of Honour book because he had left the village and in 1916 was living in Calgary, Canada. His attestation papers for the Canadian Over-seas Expeditionary Force, accurately describe his origins, his father's name, birth date, and his trade as a tobacconist.   His number was 530003. He is described as single. He was later discharged by the Canadians as unfit: but the details are sparse.

After the war an early electoral roll of Bilborough, includes him, but not with a wife. The family tree would appear to have been confused in their searches. The Electoral Roll of 1927 shows him living at The Elms, Bilborough with his brother John Henry Junior. He may have married Millicent D Clarke in the second Quarter of 1927. He died in 1975 at Falmouth in Cornwall, aged 80.

The **Raynor** families had two men of military age, both of whom served (entries **24 & 63**).

24. Stanley Raynor was visiting the Flack family at the time of the census. In 1911 he was 20 and a Railway shunter.

He may have served as a driver in the Royal Army Service Corps, service number 417026, and was treated for burned hands, 1919 10 07.

The 1939 Register places him in Leicester with his wife Eleanor and earning a living as a Railway Signalman. He is believed to have died at Leicester, 1960 06 00.

There were three families by the name of Woodhouse in Bilborough in 1911 (entries **26**, **28 & 44**)

26. Joseph Woodhouse (1881 00 00). The 1911 census described him as a farmer's son, living with his wife Edith, 33, and their infant son, Cyril, in a four roomed house in Bilborough. He enlisted in the Territorial Force to serve in the South Notts. Hussars on 1908 05 29, for one year, as a single man. The Roll of Honour book refers to him as being mobilised 1914 08 04 for Home service as a Regimental Quarter Master Sergeant in the South Notts. Hussars. He was demobilised in Sept. 1915 and released from military service for food production.

Little could be found about him after the war but this advertisement found in the Nottingham Evening Post: February 2nd, 1915, may have been placed by Joseph Woodhouse.

WAGGONER   Wanted, 21s per week, house and garden, extra harvest.- Woodhouse, Bilborough.

28. John Woodhouse at 58, a farmer, was obviously too old to be conscripted.

33. Alfred James Baines (1892 00 00) was working as a groom according to the 1911 census. He was 19 and came from Newark. He worked for the Andrews family, farmers, who owned Broxtowe Hall which was described as having 12 rooms. He was one of three servants, the other two were female. An Annie Baines was employed at Strelley Hall, also 19, and may have been his twin sister.

Broxtowe Hall had been the home of Thomas Helwys who was married at St. Martin of Tours, Bilborough and went on to be the founder of the Baptist Church.

He is not found in the Roll of Honour book and must have moved out of the village before the war. An A J Baines served as a Private in the Royal Fusiliers (London Regiment) in the 17th Service Battalion. The record refers to his admission to a sick convoy, 1918 03 15, following a gas shell attack. His service number was given as 75263 and his religion 'Church of England'.

An Alfred J Baines married Edith S Beck in Newark in 1932.

In 1911 there were two families of Hensons, one in Bilborough and the other in Strelley, of whom six were of military age (entries **36 & 67**).

36. George Henson (1887 07 26), 23, lived with his parents George, 60, and Sarah Ann (nee Parnham), 56, in the parish of Bilborough at Cinderhill and made his living as a miner according to the 1911 census. In the 1901 census, at the age of 13, he was described as a soap maker. The house had 5 rooms for the three people. In 1911 he married Lily Beatrice Hopewell in Nottingham. He very likely left his parents' home and lived elsewhere, probably Nottingham, and would therefore not have been included in the Roll of Honour book.

A George Henson enlisted in the Sherwood Foresters as a private, 1915 10 12, aged 28, and was given the service number 31577. He served until 1918 04 12, with time spent overseas, when he was declared 'no longer physically fit for war service' because of wounds and awarded the Silver War Badge, number 359127.

The next record of him is the 1939 Register where he and his wife Lily are living on the adjacent and new, Broxtowe estate, with him being described as a coal miner, 'dataller' (a labourer hired or paid by the day).

No one by the name of **Moore** was found living in Bilborough in 1881 but they went on to be significant in the village having a road named after them. The 1891 census records Samuel Moore, 21, born in Carrington, living at Chilwell Dam Farm with his maternal grandmother Charlotte Sheldon, 75. In the Rectory at Wacket Lane in Bilborough, in 1901, are found the Moore family headed by Reuben, 56, a farmer, and his wife of 42 years, Elizabeth (nee Sheldon), 54.

The 1911 census found them living at Chilwell Dam House. They had had twelve children of whom 10 were still alive, with only two resident with them, one of whom was **Albert Moore**. Recorded in the Roll of Honour book are Thomas and Albert Moore. Even though **Thomas Moore** is not recorded in the villages in 1911 he must have returned, perhaps to his parents' home, after 1911.

37. Thomas Moore (1887 09 07) joined the Royal Army Service Corps, Motor Transport as a private, service number, M2/117214 and 2117214, on Aug. 20th, 1915. He served in France from Feb. 25th, 1916 to Jan. 1919. He was present at the battle of the Somme, Aug. 1916, at Arras, 1917 and Ypres 1917. He was present at the storming of the St. Quentin Canal at Bellenglise by the Sherwood Foresters on Sept. 29th, 1918 as a driver of one of six lorries taking up ammunition. He was gassed at Gorre near Bethune and was demobilised on Jan. 27th, 1919.

His two names are so common that it was not possible to identify him from the plethora of records that the names yielded (for the 1939 Register, 2003 possibilities were obtained).

37. Albert Moore (1891 04 04), Thomas' brother, Albert, 19, was living with his parents in 1911 and was earning a living as an Engineering Apprentice (Electrical Lighting).

He joined the Sherwood Foresters in Sept. 1914 and was commissioned Mar. 22nd, 1915 and became a lieutenant on Aug. 1st, 1915, became a Captain on Nov. 17th, 1917, a major on Oct. 26th, 1918 and a Lieutenant Colonel, June 24th, 1919.

He was one of the only four men to be officers during the war: the other three came from the Edge family.

He served in France from Feb. 1st, 1916 to Nov. 1919. He saw action at Neuvechapelle, May 30th, 1916 and at the battle of the Somme, 1916. He was gassed during an attack on Ginchy and Guillemont when only 5 officers and 300 men were left out of the battalion of 800. He was also at Arras Sept. 1916. On Dec. 22nd, 1916 he joined the Tank Corps as Engineer Officer C Battalion. He was present at the battle of Arras on April 9th, 1917; Ypres, July 31st, 1917 and Cambrai, Nov. 20th, 1917. Then followed a series of appointments: second in command of Advanced Workshops; company commander main repair depot at Erin, Mar. 22nd, 1918. After the war had finished he was appointed works manager on June 24th, 1919 which involved about 57 officers, 110 white men and 2000 Chinese men employed in repairing tanks achieving a rate of 150 tanks per week.

He won the Military Cross on April 9th, 1917 and was demobilised Nov. 20th, 1919. In the Tank Corps book of honour is written T. Lieut. Moore, Albert awarded the Military Cross.

"For gallantry and devotion to duty. From March 28th to April 12th, 1917, this officer, as workshop officer to the company, worked almost continuously to keep his tanks in fighting order. The work he performed, usually in darkness under heavy shell fire, contributed greatly to the success of the operations. His fearless example has been an example to all of his subordinates".

The Nottingham Evening Post of Jan. 6th, 1916 reported that the Sherwood Foresters had been visited by the Mayor and the Sheriff, stating that: "...Drawn..........up on parade the 15th Nottingham Battalion Sherwood Foresters (the Bantams) presented a very fine appearance. ......medals to the winners of the inter-platoon football competition went to......and bronze medals...... to Lieut. A. Moore." Albert Moore was in the 15th battalion and in 1916 was a lieutenant.

38. William Moore (1875 12 15), 35, a farmer was living with his wife Elizabeth (Elizabeth Elkington whom he married 1899 05 24) at Chilwell Dam Farm and his four children, one boy and three girls, of whom the oldest was William Redvers, aged 10. In the census of 1901 he was described as a farmer and traction engine proprietor. He is not recorded in the Roll of Honour book. This may be because at the advent of conscription in 1916 it was his 41st year: 41 being the upper age limit of the 1916 acts governing conscription. He would still have been eligible in late 1918 when the age limit was raised to 51 and he would have been 43 and well within the limit. However food production was very important to beat the German blockade and as a farmer, and moreover at the forefront of mechanisation, he could well have been described as being in a reserved occupation. He probably did not move out of the village and is listed on the electoral roll of 1927 as living at Chilwell Dam Farm. The 1939 Register has him and Elizabeth living on Strelley Road in Bilborough and described as a farmer and hosiery manufacturer.

During the war a number of adverts appeared in the local newspaper, 'The Nottingham Evening Post', placed there by the Moore family.

20, 22, 23, March, 1915 MAN wanted for Farm work, able to work horses. – Moore, Bilborough, Nottingham.

04-09 October 1915 and 11-15 October 1915 SECOND Man Wanted for Threshing and Hauling Set
Moore Brothers, Bilborough, Notts

02, 04, 05, 07, 09, 11-14, October 1915 WAGGONER Wanted, house, garden and potatoes found, Character required
William Moore, Bilborough, Notts.

Friday, 15, October 1915 SEVERAL Men Wanted to assist lifting potatoes- Moore, Bilborough, Nottingham.

16-18, November, 1915 ENGINE DRIVER for Traction Threshing set, character required – Moore Bros., Bilborough, Nottingham.

29, September, 1919; 03, 04, 06, October, 1919 SALE 20 tons Wheat Straw Chop, five tons Bean Straw Chop, £6 per ton in buyers' sacks on rail Gotham sidings – Apply Wm. Moore, Bilborough, Nottingham.

The **Jackson** family had three members of an age to be called up.

39. Tom Jackson, 42, from Lincolnshire and a traction engine driver, lived with his wife Emma (nee Roberts) 37, also from Lincolnshire. They lived in a five roomed house with their four children, two boys, 14 and 11 and two girls, 7 and 1. The birth places of their children indicate that they moved from Lincolnshire, between 1900 and 1903, to live in Bilborough. At 47 years of age in 1916 Tom would have been too old to be conscripted although notionally available in 1918 at the age of 49. He is not listed in the Roll of Honour book and searches for his military history, if any, turned up 418 possible records. He is listed on the 1926 electoral register living at Moore's farm. It is almost certain that he stayed in the area and an absence of a record in the Roll of Honour book is good evidence that he did not serve.

39. Herbert Jackson (1897 00 00), 14, Tom's son, is mentioned in the Roll of Honour book. In 1911 he was living with his parents and working as a domestic groom. He volunteered as soon as he was of age.
He joined the Royal Field Artillery, 1914 12 11, as a driver and transferred to the Royal Horse Artillery Sept. 1916. He served in France from June 29th, 1915 to Nov. 30th, 1918 and was with the 'Army of Occupation in Germany' from Dec. 1918 to Oct. 1919. He saw action at Armentieres and Monchy wood in 1915 and the Somme, Vimy Ridge, Arras, and with the Canadians at Messines Ridge during 1915-1916. He was at Boessinghe, Ypres from July to October 1917. He was in

the advance on Cambrai, Nov. 1917 and at Noyon, Jan. 1918 and La Frere and Guiscard, Mar. 11th, 1918. He was in the retirement via Noyon and through the Forest of Compiegne, in reserve during the fighting around Rheims. He was in the advance from Sailley-le-Sec east of Amiens to Mont St. Quentin, Perronne on Aug. 8th, 1918 and at Sains du Nords, Nov. 11th, 1918. He advanced with the 'Army of Occupation' onto Germany via Namur and Liege. In Germany he was stationed at Dovensthoven, Bonn; Lipp, Durren and Norvenische, Cologne (Oct. 19th, 1919). He was demobilised Dec. 11th, 1920.

As with the other Jacksons his name is too common to definitively find details of him after the war.

39. Hector Jackson (1900 03 13), Herbert's brother, lived in Bilborough with his family in 1911 and was at school. His birth date would indicate that he was eligible for conscription in March 1918. He is not mentioned in the Roll of Honour book. He was living with his family in the village after the war and therefore was probably not called up, or if he was, not accepted.

As with the other Jacksons there are many records turned up by the name. He probably married Ada Robinson in 1925. He is recorded on the 1939 Register as living at the Boothyard, Nottingham with his wife Ada and earning a living as a coal merchant. He probably died at Wollaton, Nottingham, 1978 09 09.

43. George Greenham (1882 04 00) was born to John Greenham an engine driver and his wife Mary J, in Nottingham. In the 1901 census he was 19 and working as a servant, groom on a farm, to a farmer. By 1911 he had moved to Bilborough and was living with his wife at a two roomed house, North Lodge, Bilborough Lane and was earning his living as a Woodman on the estate. George had married Annie Dobney, born in Crowland, Lincolnshire, 1910, who was almost certainly the sister of **George Dobney (43)**, see earlier.

The Roll of Honour book has him re-joining the Sherwood Foresters (Territorial) as a private on Nov. 29th, 1915, service numbers 4493 and 306474. No earlier service was found. He served in France June 6th, 1916 to Feb. 24th, 1919. He saw action at the battle of the Somme; Lens April 27th, 1917 and Loos, Aug. 23rd, 1917. He was at Bellenglise where he swam the St. Quentin canal, Sept. 1918. He was in action at the villages of Montbrehain and Bohain, Oct. 4th, 1918, and in the joint action with the French, Oct. 17th, 1918 when the Forest of Audigny was taken. He was wounded in the head at Gorre, but the date is not given. He was demobilised 1919 02 24.

He died shortly after the war, 1925 Q3, in Nottingham: he was 42.

The Woodhouse family lived in Bilborough and consisted of John Woodhouse, 61, and his sons John and Archibald and his grandsons William and Eric Burton.

44. John Woodhouse, (1880 00 00), single, was described as a general labourer on a farm. That farm was likely to be the Old Rectory farm where William was resident with his grandparents John and Catherine Woodhouse. These people were the parents of John who was baptised at St. Martin of Tours, Bilborough, 1880 08 29. Searches for his military history threw up 116 possible records: he is not mentioned in the Roll of Honour book.

44. Archibald Thomas Woodhouse (1886 07 17), 24, John's younger brother, also lived at Old Rectory farm with his parents. He was described as a 'dataller in mine'. No record could be found of military service and he has no record in the Roll of Honour book.

After the war he married Muriel H Kirk in Nottingham in 1923. The 1939 Register describes him as a 'Tobacco worker' living at 133, Forest Road West, Nottingham with his wife Muriel. He died in 1970 at Nottingham, aged 83.

The following advert was found in the local paper, The Nottingham Evening Post, and may have been placed there by the Woodhouses of Rectory Farm.

February 2nd, 1915. WAGGONER Wanted, 21s per week, house and garden, extra harvest.- Woodhouse, Bilborough.

This may indicate a shortage of farm labour due to the mobilisation of Joseph Woodhouse in August, 1915, and may be why he was released from military service to aid in food production. It may also be the reason that his brother was not conscripted. He may by the war years have left mining and returned to working the farm with his parents.

44. William Burton, (1900 00 00). In 1911 he was a schoolboy and lived with his grandparents, John, 61, a miner, and Catherine Woodhouse and Annie Frances Burton, his mother. They lived in a five roomed house, probably in Bilborough Lane, shared with five adults and his younger brother. Searches turned up 399 military records, none of which could be specifically attributed to him. A William Laurence Burton was baptised at St. Martin of Tours, Bilborough, on 1900 05 13. His parents were John Andrew and Annie Frances Burton who lived in Bulwell. If this was the William in question he was clearly born in the first quarter of 1900 and would therefore have been eligible for conscription in the first quarter of 1918.

46. Frederick G Sly (1876 05 18) was born in Strelley to Robert Sly (d. 1902), from Eastington, Gloucestershire and his wife Annie (b. 1850) also from Eastington. In 1901 Frederick was living in Strelley, working as a woodman, labouring, and living with his widowed mother and two older sisters.

In 1911 he was living on Strelley Lane with his family in a three roomed house. His occupation was now as a carter for the colliery. His mother did domestic work and one sister was a dressmaker and the other a hosiery machinist. In 1914 Ann Sly paid rent of £1 15s per half year (Estate Rent book).

The document recording his award of a 'Silver War Badge' showed he enlisted in the Sherwood Foresters as a Private, 1915 07 13, service number 27997. He was discharged 1916 05 18 and had not served overseas. His badge number was 74497 and issued 1916 12 09. The cause of discharge was sickness: paragraph 392 King's Regulations (xvi), no longer physically fit for war service.

It is not clear why he was not mentioned in the Roll of Honour book and the conclusion must be that he left the village and was living elsewhere.

He probably married Eliza J Smith in the fourth quarter of 1921 the marriage being recorded at the Basford office.

In the 1939 Register he was still living in Strelley Lane, Strelley with his wife Eliza A, and working as a Canal Ganger and on Railway Engineering, described as main and repair staff and the work (heavy).

47. Edward Simpkin (1870 02 00) was born, in Bilborough, to Martin, a coal miner from Paston in Northamptonshire and Mary Ann from Kimberley. In 1871 Martin was a farm labourer and Edward, 11, at school. By 1881 Martin was a widower and a farm labourer, with the Musgroves and the Stevensons as neighbours, and Edward had become a coal miner.

On 1893 11 26 Edward joined the Sherwood Foresters, 4th Battalion, service number 4892: he was 23 years and 9 months of age and living in Bilborough. This must have been a short service attestation, because, in 1901, Edward was a coal miner living with his father Martin and still single.

He married Mary about 1904 and by the 1911 census had three children, a boy, 5, and two girls, 3 and 1: all born in Nottingham. They lived in a three roomed house on Strelley Lane, but by now Edward was a farm labourer and 41 years old.

No further service record was found for him. He would have been 46 in 1916 and beyond the age of conscription but within the upper limit of 51 in 1918.

He probably died in Nottingham in 1924 aged 54.

The **Stevenson** family had four men of military age in the two villages (entries **49 & 65**).

49. Frank Stevenson (1880 10 19) was living with his parents Charles, 53, a miner from Strelley, his mother Mary Hannah (nee Smedley), 55, from Bramcote, and two brothers and a sister at Strelley Lane, Strelley. He was a machine fitter. He was still with his parents in 1911 sharing a four roomed house with them and two younger sisters. His parents had been married for 39 years and had had seven children all of them living. He was still a machine fitter, with one of his sisters a dress maker and the other a shop assistant. His father paid a half yearly rent of £1 5s for the house (Estate Rent register).

There were many military records for the name Frank Stevenson. The following is a possibility.

He joined the Sherwood Foresters, 1914 11 14 as a private, service number 19119. He served to 1918 02 10 when he was discharged because of sickness, as no longer physically fit for war service, and awarded a Silver War Badge, number

207489. He was not listed in the Roll of Honour book and either did not serve or had moved away.

He is described on the 1939 Register as single, an engineer's fitter (heavy work) and living in Nottingham. It showed that he had moved away although it is not clear when. His parents were old in 1911, 63 and 65 respectively, and their possible deaths over the next few years may have generated a move.

50. John Phillip (1893 00 00). He was born in London and in 1911 was working for a farmer, William Carrington Horner (53) from Kettering, and his wife Eliza (42) from Lincolnshire. He worked as a farm milking hand (aged 18) along with Thomas Oaglen and lived with the Horners at Catstone Hill Farm, Strelley (10 rooms).

He is not recorded in the Roll of Honour book and so must have moved on by the start of the war. It was difficult to find a definitive war record for him but the following may fit.

The details are taken from discharge papers which put his service record from 1916 09 21 to 1918 09 17. He had served in the Royal Field Artillery, 3c Reserve brigade as a gunner, service number 171689, and his age given as 24. This may have been a year too young for him, but the recording of a person's age may not have been precise, either in the Census or army records. The particulars were furnished in Woolwich and the reason for his discharge was given as wounds, not physically fit for war service, and he was awarded a Silver War Badge.

It was not possible to find definitive information about his discharge from the army.

The **Dunmores** had two men of military age (see **51 and 83**) and a third William (see **83**) who was 10 in the census of 1911, a third possibility.

No Dunmores are recorded in the Roll of Honour book. George, 54, (farm labourer) and Matilda Dunmore, 50, had been married for 28 years in 1911 and had had 12 children of whom 11 were living. They lived in a five roomed house with four of their children, two boys, 19 and 10 and two girls, 16 and 11. A further son, Walter, 14, lived as a farm servant at Rectory Farm, Strelley, helping an elderly spinster, Elizabeth Price, 72, run the farm. George came from Northants and Matilda, Lincolnshire. All of their children in the 1911 census were recorded as being born in Lincolnshire and they, therefore, must have come to Strelley after 1901.

51. Walter Dunmore (1898 07 00), was born at Little Ponton, Lincolnshire, to George and Matilda. In 1911 he was 14 and living at Rectory farm with the owner, a farmer and grazier, Elizabeth Price. He was described as a farm labourer. He was probably not living with his family, which was large, in a house which was small, but at Rectory Farm where there were 6 rooms for two people.

It is likely that he joined the Sherwood Foresters. Information about him is thin on the ground, but a medal index record has a Walter Dunmore in that regiment, as a private, service number 61245.

Post war data is almost non-existent and he is not found in the 1939 Register. A family tree record had him emigrating to St. Johns, New Brunswick, 1929 01 12.

The **Edge** family were rich land owners. Thomas Edge bought the estates of the Strelley family, in 1678, which included the parishes of Strelley and Bilborough.

The squire, in 1911, was Thomas Lewis Kekewich Edge, aged 55, and his wife of the same age, Frances Etheldreda. They had 7 children, 4 girls and 3 boys. All three of the boys joined the army, each one as an officer: only one other of the parish men joined as an officer (Albert Moore, **37**). Many of the people who are the subjects of this book worked directly or indirectly for the Edges or lived in one of their tied cottages which are listed in the 'Estate Rent Book'. T L K Edge was also a JP and as such sat on committees judging whether men should be exempt, receive a pension etc. He is frequently mentioned in the local paper, some 52 entries were found between 1916 and 1918 alone.

One advertisement in the Nottingham Evening Post, Saturday, 09 March 1918 read:

"Discharged Soldier or ineligible Man Wanted to help in private Garage and Garden, unmarried man preferred – Edge, Strelley Hall, Nottingham."

This would indicate that he thought all able bodied men should be serving but also a preparedness to help those who had and in doing so had suffered.

The Post in reporting on him, 1916 03 15, referred to him as Major Edge.

53. James Vernon (b. 1889 10 12) is recorded in the 1901 census as boarding at The Grange School in Hoddesdon with his older brother Ralph and 11 other boys aged 9-13. In 1911 he was a boarder at Wye in Kent where he was an agricultural student. He was the first of the Edges to enlist and was gazetted as a lieutenant into the Sherwood Foresters on October 2nd, 1914. Apart from the Roll of Honour book little can be found of his service record and that in the book is a little thin. He served in France, Feb. 27th, 1915 until Dec. 8th, 1915 and was in action at Hooge July, 1915 and at the Hohenzollern Redoubt, Oct. 1915. On May 9th, 1915 he was slightly wounded and severely wounded on Oct. 14th, 1915. He was discharged as unfit for service on Feb. 23rd, 1918.

In 1915 the Nottingham Evening Post published the following notice of the wounded:

"Lieut. James V Edge who has been wounded in action, is a son of Mr. T. L. K. Edge of Strelley. He received a commission in the 8th Battalion, Sherwood Foresters in October of last year, and was promoted to a full lieutenancy four months ago. He was a member of Captain Ashwell's company".

His record in the intervening years is unknown but given that his wounds were severe, it is likely that he spent the intervening period of time in Britain either in hospital or with light duties, or both, until his discharge.

The electoral roll of 1925 found him resident at Quarry House (very near to the Hall) in Strelley. He appears to have married Rachel M Young at Hexham in 1921. The 1939 Register shows him to be living with Rachel at Red House, Maltersey Rd.,

Ranskill, Retford and earning his living as a Farm & Chartered Land agent. He died in June 1971, aged 81, in Cockermouth in Cumberland.

Staff outside Strelley Hall 1905   Photograph courtesy of Mrs M Henshell

Fig. 28 Staff of Strelley Hall in 1905

53. His older brother **Ralph Thomas** (1888 09 23) was at the same school as James Vernon according to the 1901 census and was living at Strelley Hall with his parents in 1911, and listed as a student. In 1914 (Feb. 11th) he was proposed for the Institute of Civil Engineers. At the time he was still living at Strelley Hall. It can be deduced that he spent his time at some college or institute studying the subject and either gaining admission to the ICE on the basis of that qualification or by passing some entrance examination of ICE. Either way it appears he was a qualified civil engineer at the start of the war and therefore it is no surprise that he enlisted in the Royal Engineers and was gazetted as a temporary lieutenant on April 25th, 1915. He served Aug. – Dec. 1915 in France before joining the Egyptian Expeditionary Force.

He was awarded the Military Cross as 'Ralph Thomas Edge, Temporary Lieutenant. Gazette Number 6490, 03/06/1918, for an act or acts of exemplary gallantry during operations against the enemy'. Operations in Egypt included Sollum, at the engagement at Agadir on 26/02/1916.

During November and December 1917 he took part in operations to take Beesheba and Jerusalem. He commanded a company of the Royal Engineers in the final destruction of the Turkish armies in Syria, Sept. 1918. He was demobilised Sept. 12th, 1919 by which time he had been promoted to Captain.

Not a lot is known about him after the war. He married Gladys Marr Torr at Eastham in Cheshire in 1919. The 1939 Register describes him as a Civil Engineer Director Comping and living at Ivy House, Buckingham, alone but for a Rosa M Homewood. He died in 1972 at Midhurst in Sussex, aged 84.

53. The youngest brother **Roger Francis** (1897 10 15) is not recorded in the 1911 census as being with his parents at Strelley Hall. He would have been 13 and probably away at boarding school. Whether he volunteered or was conscripted on his 18th birthday is not known but was gazetted Aug. 28th, 1916, aged 18, into the Coldstream Guards. He served in France from Jan. 21st, 1917 and was at Ypres and Cambrai in 1917, in the Arras sector Mar. 1918 and Manbeuge, Nov. 9th, 1918. After the war he moved to Cologne on Dec. 23rd, 1918.

In Nov. 1917 he was awarded the Military Cross, which was reported twice in the local Nottingham Evening Post.

Firstly on 18 March 1918. "The Investiture by the King in London on Saturday Lieut. Roger Francis Edge, Coldstream Guards, received his Military Cross, and his sister, Miss N. C. S. Edge was present, representing the Notts. Detachment of the Women's Legion Motor Drivers at the inspection of the King. They are the youngest son and daughter of Mr and Mrs Edge of Strelley Hall."

Secondly on Saturday 27 April 1918 "NOTTS. OFFICERS' MILITARY CROSS Lieut. Roger Francis Edge, Coldstream Guards, youngest son of Mr. and Mrs. Edge of Strelley Hall received the Military Cross. For conspicuous gallantry and devotion to duty whilst engaged with a party in carrying and fixing duck boards. Although his men were continually dispersed by shell fire and many casualties caused, he rallied them again and completed his task."

He was demobilised in Dec. 14th, 1919

On Oct. 8th, 1926 he sailed to Colombo, Ceylon aboard the "Mantola" of the British India Shipping & Navigation Company, Ltd. as a 2nd class passenger. He was described as 28 and an assistant, not accompanied by a wife, with his last address, the Guards Club, Brook Street. He is then recorded as returning aboard the "Reina Del Pacifico", of the Pacific Steam Navigation Co., with an official number of 162339, bound for Liverpool. He arrived in Liverpool 1945 06 10. He was described as 47 and a Merchant, with his address as, c/o Thatdred House Club, St James SW.

He died in May 1984 at Haywards Heath, Sussex, aged 86.

53. Herbert Dawn (1892 00 00). He was born to John, a yardsman on a farm and Elizabeth at Witton in the Vale, Nottinghamshire and baptised 1892 06 20. In 1911 he was working as a valet at Strelley Hall.

He enlisted at Cowley Barracks into the Regimental Training Reserve, 96th Battalion, service number 378186 (also 17723), 1917 06 10 when he was 25 and 1 month old. His father is given as John Dawn of 24, Church Row, Witton in the

Vale. His residence was given as Blenheim Palace, Woodstock and his occupation as valet. He was described as 5' 6.5" tall, chest 32" with an expansion of 4" and having as a distinctive mark, an appendix scar. His medical classification was B1. Records show that he embarked 1917 09 30 (although to where is not stated) and disembarked 1917 10 02. He was listed on a casualty form. He was transferred to the Labour Corps. and was demobilised 1920 02 12. He may have been posted as a valet, to a senior army officer, given his medical classification and the length of time to demobilisation.

No marriage record could be found. In 1939 he was working in London at 25 Cliveden Place, Chelsea with his occupation described as domestic duties. He died in Westminster, London in September, 1941, aged 49.

There were three Stevensons in the villages.

62. Samuel Stevenson (1871 04 00) was the oldest and in 1911 was living with his parents, Samuel and Sarah Ann Stevenson, in a house with 4 rooms and listed with a rent of £2 per half year in the 1911 Estate book. He was single and a miner. Very little can be found for him because of the large number of Samuel Stevensons turned up in searches. It is unlikely that he served since he was too old at the introduction of conscription in 1916 and would have been 47 in 1918.

62. Frank Stevenson (1873 04 29) the next oldest son, married Alice Whitely in 1897. The 1911 census recorded them as having two children, both living. They lived on the Bridle Road in Strelley in a house with four rooms and he was described as a miner. The house was a tied cottage and the Estate book of 1911 records the rent as £3 5s for each half year. He was born in Strelley and Alice in the adjacent town of Kimberley. They were still living in the village, at the Gate House at Swingate (on the Bridle Road), according to the 1939 Register, with Frank described as a retired miner (he would have been 65). Since he was almost certainly resident in the village over the course of the war, and is not recorded in the Roll of Honour book, it is most likely that he did not serve.

62. The youngest **Simeon Stevenson** (1898 01 01) definitely served and is mentioned in the Roll of Honour book. He was the son of Frank and Alice Stevenson and in the 1911 census he was 13 and living with his parents and younger brother at the Gate House on the Bridle Road in Strelley. The house had four rooms and he was described as a pony driver at a colliery.

The Roll of Honour book records him as enlisting as a Guardsman in the Coldstream Guards on April 23rd, 1918. He was trained at Caterham and Windsor, was put on Home service, and demobilised Dec. 14th, 1918. Other records have him enlisting in the Coldstream Guards, service number 25603, on 1916 02 19 when he was 18 years and 1 month old. His address is given as the Gate House, Strelley.

A further 'Descriptive Report on Enlistment', undated, describes him as aged 20 years and 4 months old: this would therefore have been May 1918. His address is given as the Gate House, Strelley and his father named as Frank. He was 5' 8.5" with a chest measurement of 39" and an expansion of 3". His religion was that of Primitive Methodist (there was a chapel in nearby Babbington).

Little was found about him after the war, but he is recorded in the 1939 Register as Simon, living at Mcfarland Terrace, Nottingham with his wife Elizabeth and working as a colliery hewer. It is likely that he married Elizabeth A Holmes in 1925 and died in 1959.

63. Joseph Frederick Raynor (1889 00 00), 21, a coal porter (above ground) was living with his parents William, 67, a miner and contractor and hewer (a butty?) and Matilda, 58, in a 5 roomed house on the Bridle Road in Strelley. His military papers record that in 1915 he was still living on the Bridle Road, with his parents and working as a gardener.

He is listed in the Roll of Honour book. He joined the Sherwood Foresters as a private on Feb. 24th, 1916, initially in the 11th Battalion but was transferred to the 2/7th with a service number 36614. He saw action at Hill 60 on the Ypres Salient April 9th, 1917. He was wounded in the right shoulder and leg at Lonnebeke Sept. 26th, 1917. He was wounded severely in the right arm and left leg and was discharged from the army 1918 04 16. He was awarded the Silver War Badge, number: 402602.

Definitive records were difficult to find for him after the war. He may have married Margaret Wood 4Q, 1918. A Joseph F (born 1890) died in 1949. The death was registered in Basford and would indicate that he was still living in Strelley or Bilborough at the time of his death.

60. Samuel Morley (1878 00 00). He was born in Kimberley to Samuel and Eliza. In 1891 he was living with his parents, Samuel, a coal miner, and his mother and their family in Kimberley. He was 13 years old and a coal miner. By 1901 his father had become a grocer (shopkeeper) and he was now an insurance agent for the Prudential. He married Ada Barker from Strelley in the third quarter of 1909. By 1911 he was living at Old Park Farm (9 rooms) with his wife, Ada, and his in laws James and Susannah Barker and still working as an insurance agent.

No definitive record of military service was found for him and he is not recorded in the Roll of Honour book. He and Ada can be found on the electoral rolls of 1921 and 1922 and it is therefore probable that he did not leave the village. Given his early death in the first quarter of 1925 (b. 1878) aged 47 it may have been that he was in poor health and failed the army medical. The change from earning a living from coal miner to insurance agent was possibly prompted by ill health.

69. Charles Headland (1881 07 20). He was born at Honington, Lincolnshire to Charles and Frances. The 1901 census describes him as a farmer's son. He married Lily Ann Walton in the second quarter of 1909 with the marriage register in

Newark. By 1911, he was living with his wife Lily (32), also from Lincolnshire, at Hall Farm Cottages (5 rooms) with their daughter Alice Mary (1) and Lily Walton, aged 11, from London. He was employed as the head waggoner on a farm. He is not recorded in the Roll of Honour book and had probably left the village.

A very likely military record has him as 38 and as a driver in the Royal Garrison Artillery, 18th Heavy Battalion, service number 201868. He had three years and three months service and had been with the field force for two years. He was diagnosed with malaria in 1918 07 26, and was transferred to a sick convoy, 1918 07 27. His calculated date of enlistment would have been April 1915.

The 1939 Register records him living with Lilian at 40, Burrows Avenue, Beeston and earning a living as a gardener and general labourer, described as heavy work. He died in September 1962 (b.1880), aged 84, the death being reistered at Basford.

Buggart House (Keeper's Cottage)
Swingate Farm
Demolished 1956

Photograph courtesy Mrs K Blant

Fig. 29 Boggart House probably number 63 in the 1911 Census

70. Arthur Powell (1887 00 00) was born in Monmouth, Wales and in 1911 was working as an under gardener (at Strelley Hall?). He was boarding with Kate Lauder, her young daughter and three adult male boarders. Kate lived at Hall Farm which had five rooms, which would have meant crowded sleeping conditions for the men.

Searching for records for him was difficult because of the lack of refining details. He, however, may have been Arthur Henry Powell who joined the Royal Army Service Corps, 13th Mechanical Transport Co.: service number M2/167102. A pension claims form records those details and that he was 32, born 1887 at Monmouth, at the time of the completion of the form, 1919.

He was resident in East Bridgeford and may have married a Mary Keightley, 1912, in Nottingham.

70. A fellow boarder at Hall Farm with Kate Lauder was **Harry Samways** (1892 00 00). He was an odd job man at the Hall and had been born at Norbury in Derbyshire. The 1901 census describes him as Harry S Samways.

A form for the award of a 'Silver War Badge', number B56789, may be his. It records a Harry Samways, aged 23, details his service to 1918 12 03, and this may be the date taken, or thereabouts, for the award. He had been in the Royal Field Artillery, 232 Brigade, as a driver, service number, 810690 with service from 1913 01 21. The age of 23 in 1918 would make him 16 in 1911 (19 in the census).

A Harry S Samways, born 1890, died Sept. 1950 in Derby, aged 60.

70. The 1901 census for **George Wallbank** (1890 02 12), gives his father as Fred, his mother as Elizabeth and he as George W.

In 1911 he was boarding with Harry Samways, Arthur Powell and William Sullivan at Hall Farm, five rooms, with Kate Lauder in Staffordshire. William Sullivan, 47, was from Deptford, London and described as a house painter and church decorator. 1911 was the year that the chancel ceiling was painted in the local church.

Only a few records were found for war service for a George Wallbank and only one seemed to fit. A George Wilfred Wallbank was awarded the Silver War Badge, 1919 02 10. He had enlisted in the West Riding Regiment as a private, 1917 04 10, service number 32690, and served overseas. He was discharged from the army, 1918 11 18 because of wounds, army order VI, aged 28. He probably moved out of the village, possibly back to the West Midlands, and as such would not be recorded in the Roll of Honour book.

After the war the 1939 Register records him living in Birmingham, with his wife S Wallbank, and her daughter. He was 21, working as an under gardener with his birth place given as Bircheshead working as an upholsterer. He may have died in Birmingham 1960 12 00.

73. In 1911, **William Panton Barnes** (1876 02 04) a domestic gardener from Stanfield in Lincolnshire lived at The Gardens, Strelley Hall with his wife Henrietta (Maidment) 36, from Ebberstone Yorkshire. They had been married at South Kilvington, 1900 03 06 and had one child, with the same name as his father, aged 3, and born in Naburn, Yorks. The house had 3 rooms, 1 down, two up. He is not listed in the Roll of Honour book probably because he moved back to Yorkshire before the war.

A military record shows that the Royal Air Force engaged him 1918 05 30 aged 42 years and 3 months and gave him the service number 190575. He was transferred to the Royal Air Force Reserve 1919 02 28 and discharged 1920 04 30.

His trade was given as gardener and his religion 'Church of England'. He was described as 5' 7" with a 32" chest. His hair was brown, eyes blue, and with a sallow complexion. Her address is given as 6 Red Cross Terrace, Brough, East Yorkshire.

He died in Frome, Somerset, 1944 06 24.

The **Smith** family in the village had four men of military age 1914-1918 (entries **76 & 81**).

76. Jesse Harry Smith (1875 00 00) was born in Cranfield, Bedfordshire. In 1911 he was living, in Strelley, with his wife Fanny (nee Hammond) from Skegby, Nottinghamshire and working as a farm labourer. They had been married 17 years and had had 11 children of which eight had survived. Six, all girls, were living with them in a five roomed house. In 1916 he would have been 41 and therefore only a possibility for conscription, although eligible in 1918. With a surname like Smith many records would be available, and even with first names like Jesse Harry, 198 possibilities were found.

A Jesse Smith who had been born in 1876, died June, 1925 at Bingham, Nottinghamshire.

81. James Smith (1877 10 28) was born to George, a farm labourer, and Rebecca in Bilborough and christened at St Martin of Tours. He married Elizabeth Stevenson in 1898 07 16 and in 1901 he was living with her, two young sons and his brother Mark, 22, a farm labourer, in Bilborough. He was a waggoner on a farm. At the 1911 census they were living with their four children three boys 12, 10, 7 and one girl, 6, in Bilborough in a four roomed house which was a tied cottage, recorded in the Estate Rent register as having a rent of £3 half yearly. James is described as a carter at a colliery and married for 12 years and had had five children of whom four were living. His absence from the Roll of Honour book would suggest that he had moved out of the village.

Searches of military records yielded over 4000 records, of which around 50 could have fitted James. However the following record has sufficient cross references to suggest that it was James.

The record refers to a James Smith born in 1877 and 39 at the time of the discharge record in 1916. The discharge was from the 18th Battalion of the Sherwood Foresters, service number 28913, and took place at Woking, 1916 03 18, with the county of his residence given as Nottinghamshire. He was described as 5' tall with a chest of 32" with an expansion of 12!. His complexion was fresh, eyes blue, hair black and grey and with a scar on his left forearm. He was discharged in consequence of: Para 392 (III) (cc) King's Regulations, 'not being likely to become an efficient soldier (on Medical Grounds)'. Aldershot TMB

24/02/1916. His military character was described as fair. His trade was given as labourer and he lived at 34 Poplar St., off London Road, Nottingham.

It was not possible to find out much about him after the war because of the number of Smiths generated in searches but the '1939 Register' has him living on Main Road, Bilborough with his wife Elizabeth, b. 1878 02 07. He was born 1877 10 06 and in 1939 was incapacitated. A James Smith died 1Q, 1963, b. 1877, aged 86. Another James Smith, also b. 1877, died in 1958, aged 81.

81. Harry Smith (1898 07 17) was born in Bilborough to James Smith, a waggoner on a farm, born in Bilborough, and Elizabeth (nee Stevenson) in Strelley and baptised at All Saints Church, Strelley, 1898 09 11. The 1901 census has them living on Main Road, Bilborough.

With common names like Harry and Smith it was always going to be difficult to find definitive records for him. The various sources of military service yielded 3-4000 possible records. Since he was not listed in the Roll of Honour book it could be concluded that he had moved out of the village or not served. He would have been eligible for conscription in 1917 and with the demand for men to pursue the war it is unlikely that an eighteen year old would be overlooked. It could be that he was one of those who were physically unfit, or that his family had left the villages. His mother, Elizabeth, died in 1913 and it is therefore very possible that his father moved on. However In 1914 his father, James, was paying rent of £3 per half year (Estate Rent register)

A possibility is Harry Smith who joined the Sherwood Foresters, 52nd, 53rd (Graduated) Battalion, service number TR/6/52922, in 1918. His residence was given as Carlton, Nottingham and his occupation, coal miner. He was single, born in 1900 and aged 18. The attestation form is stamped with a medical category of A. Much of this fitted him but for the age.

According to the '1939 Register' he was living at Grange Cottage and working as a horseman and cowman, described as heavy work. He was born, 1898 07 17 and was living with his wife Mary G, b. 1897 and an Emily J. Nash, b. Dec. 1860. A family history tree describes him marrying a Mary Gwendoline Ruth Nash and dying in 1969. A Harry Smith died 1970 04 12 (b. 1898 07 17), the death was registered in Basford.

83. John Thomas Dunmore (1893 05 29) was described as a farm labourer in the 1911 census. Records of the Royal Navy, has a John Thomas Dunmore serving aboard HMS Victory II, having enlisted in 1911 06 27 and leaving 1923 06 28 from the same ship. His service number was K11610. He served in a number of ships, in sequence they were Victory II; Renown; Pathfinder; Victory II, Hyacinth and Victory II. His character was described over the years as good or very good and his ability moderate to satisfactory in the early years, and superior in the later years. He received a war gratuity, 1919 12 31. He was described as 5' 3.5" tall with brown hair, blue eyes and a fresh complexion. He was born in Grantham, 1893 05 29 and his occupation was described as a farm labourer. The 1911 census has him aged 19 on the day of the census April 2nd: If the naval records are correct he would have been 17. The 1911 census has him born in Lincolnshire at West Deeping which is some way from Grantham. The 1901 census places the birth at Skillington which is very close to Grantham and his age as 2, which is consistent with the 1911 census. With the facts available, but with the exception of the age discrepancy, they are consistent with the John Thomas of the village, and would explain why he was not listed in the Roll of Honour book, since he left the village in 1911.

A further possibility is a J Dunmore who was a private in the Field Artillery, service number 22575, who caught influenza in 1918 as a 26 year old. He had completed four years of service and had been with the field force for 3 years. He was transferred to a sick convoy 1918 11 12. His religion was recorded as Church of England. All of the available information fits for John Thomas but there are too few cross references to be absolutely sure.

No obvious post-war information was found for him.

83. The youngest member **William Dunmore** (1901 00 00) also born in Little Ponton was 10, and at school, at the time of the 1911 census (April 2nd). No military record has been found for him. If he was 10 just before the census was taken he would have been too young to have been conscripted. If he was 11 just after the taking of the census he would have been eligible. No evidence of his exact date of birth was available.

88. James Faulconbridge (1890 11 19), 20, was an engineman at a colliery. He was living with his parents, Joseph, 44, a stoker at a colliery, and Henrietta, 38, at the Post Office in Strelley village, Fig. 32. His parents had been married for 20 years and Joseph was their only child.

He is listed in the Roll of Honour book. He was attested, 1915 12 15, aged 22, into the Sherwood Foresters, although it does not mention the rank on joining. He ultimately became a Quarter Master Sergeant in the 1/6th Battalion (Territorial) with the service numbers 7737, 242527, Fig. 33. He joined for service, 1916 04 16, and served in France from January,
1917 to 1919. He was in action at Lens and was present at the attack on Bellenglise across the St. Quentin Canal on Sept. 29th, 1918 and the attack on Ramicourt Oct. 3rd, 1918. After the armistice he was transferred to a German 'Prisoner of War Company' at Lieramont and Epeky and was engaged in clearing up the devastated area. He was demobilised Sept. 3rd, 1919.

During the war he married Agnes M Skerry, 1916, who was a servant at Strelley Hall. The wedding photograph of James, Fig. 34, shows a cross section of the villagers including the rector, Benjamin Williams, in 1916.

A James Faulconbridge died in 1969, and if him, he would have been 79.

Fig. 30 House probably number 82 in the 1911 Census

Fig. 31 Cottages probably numbers 86 & 87 in the 1911 Census

THE FOLLOWING ARE THE MEN NOT RECORDED IN THE 1911 CENSUS AND WHO SURVIVED THE WAR

A number of the men recorded in the Roll of Honour book were not living in the either of the villages in 1911. Since they are recorded in the Roll of Honour book they must have moved into the village after the Census. The date and places they lived are unknown. Their records follow.

The **Appleyard** brothers came to the village after 1911. In 1911 they lived with their parents, John George, 48, a farmer from Lincolnshire and Jane 44, from Nottinghamshire: within the household were 7 children: 5 boys; 4 sons 3, 9, 13, 17 and a nephew, 20; two daughters, 9 and 14 and a male servant 15. The house had 10 rooms. George was the 13 year old and described as 'farmer's son working on farm'. Henry was still at school.

George Appleyard (1898 00 00) enlisted Dec. 8th, 1915 as a private in the Sherwood Foresters. He served in Belgium and France from June 20th, 1916 to Feb. 1918 where he saw action on the Somme. He was demobilised Feb. 6th, 1919. The Roll of Honour book has only this information about him and other sources provide only his service number, 49053.

He may have married Eliza Caulton in 1919. He is not reported in the 1939 Register.

An article in the Nottingham Evening Post of Wednesday Aug. 7th, 1918 may well have related to the Appleyard family. "A young soldier named Bernard Marriott, who belongs to Whitby, was sentenced to 14 days' hard labour at Nottingham Shire Hall today for a theft of clothing. Prisoner, who was handed over to the military in 1917 after being charged for larceny, deserted. He went to Strelley and told Mr Appleyard, a farmer, that he was on furlough and wanted work on the land. After being given work he took some clothing belonging to two other men but was apprehended before he could dispose of it."

Henry Appleyard (1900 06 27) joined the Royal Navy on 1918 09 11 as a stoker second class, service number K53753. He saw duty in the North Sea with patrols in the light cruiser Victory. After the armistice the Victory escorted two German submarines to Portsmouth. He was demobilised 1919 03 12.

No definitive records were found for him after the war.

Cornelius Mann (1892 11 07) was born at Docking, Norfolk to John Mann, a farmer, and his wife, Charlotte. In the 1901 census he lived with his parents at Chalk Farm, New Houghton, Norfolk with five of his brothers and sisters. By 1911 he had moved to Beeston, Nottinghamshire, where he was a boarder with the Mears family and working as a labourer in a nursery. The house had five rooms and with the couple, two adult male boarders and three children the house would be crowded.

At some point he must have moved into Bilborough/Strelley as he is included in the Roll of Honour book. His title is rather lengthy, reading that he enlisted Nov. 10th, 1915 as a private in the Royal Army Service Corps, Motor Transport, Ammunition Column attached to the 129 Siege battery, Royal Garrison Artillery, service number M2/148122. He served in France and Germany and then with the Army of Occupation from July 29th, 1916 to April 28th, 1919. He saw action on the Somme and at Arras, Armentieres, Ypres, Peronne and Menin. He was demobilised May 1st, 1919 and transferred to the Reserve, May 29th, 1919.

Little was found about him after the war. He may have married Leah Taylor in the third quarter of 1919 at Wisbech. He was recorded in the 1939 Register at Glen Holt, Newark earning his living as a poultry farmer.

In 1901 William Pearson, a Coal Merchants Manager, and his wife Jessie B lived in Nottingham. In 1911 they were living in a seven roomed house at Lenton Boulevard, Nottingham with their three children of whom Thomas W, was the oldest. William was now a Farm Manager and Jessie B was a shopkeeper. They were comfortably off, with a sizeable house and a servant.

Strelley Post Office (sign mid-right of house) home to Joseph and Henrietta Faulconbridge and in 1911 to their son James (Roll of Honour)

Fig. 32 The Post Office probably number 88 in the 1911 Census

Thomas William Pearson (1900 04 02) was still at school. At some point the family would have moved into one of the two parishes. His military career described in the Roll of Honour book is necessarily short. He joined the Royal Air Force on June 12th, 1918 as a Cadet, was trained at Hastings and Reading and did Home Service. He was demobilised on Jan. 17th, 1919.

The family placed several advertisements in the Nottingham Evening Post

April 4th, 1919 LOST, at Bilborough, March 31st, Black Oilskin Coat, finder rewarded, - Pearson, Strelley

May 27th and 28th, 1919 WAGGONER Wanted, good all-round man, cottage and garden found – Pearson, Strelley

The latter two would indicate that William was still a Farm Manager or possibly running his own farm.

Fig. 33 James Faulconbridge in uniform

Thomas William Pearson married Frances M Allen in 1930. This is probably the daughter of John William Allen (Frances May) who lived at the Elms in 1911 when she was three years old. From the 1939 Register we know that he was living in West Bridgford, Nottinghamshire with Frances and was earning his living as a Milk Retailer.

He died 1974 12 29 aged 74, his death being recorded at the Rushcliffe office.

The Shipstone family were all born in Bulwell. In 1901 it was headed by **Edward Shipstone**, 29, a bricklayer and his wife Elizabeth 26. They had two children aged 6 and 2. In 1911 he had become an Innkeeper at 'The Cricketer's Arms' in Awsworth. His family had expanded to six children, four daughters and two sons. The Inn offered him accommodation of eight rooms. He would have been too old to be conscripted in 1916 (aged 44) but would have been eligible in 1918 when he would have been 46. He is not mentioned in the Roll of Honour book and may have been living elsewhere or did not serve.

Joseph Ewart Shipstone (1897 05 19, possibly 1898 08 19) Edward's son, was 12 in 1911, living with his parents in Awsworth, and still at school. Subsequently either he alone, or with his parents, moved to either Bilborough or Strelley villages. Records give some confusion as to his date of birth which is likely to be 1898 since the census of 1911 has him as twelve years of age. In April 1911 he could only have been twelve if he had been born after April 1911.

The Roll of Honour book details him joining the Royal Garrison Artillery as a Gunner on June 1st, 1918. He was trained at Aldershot and sailed from Southampton on Sept. 9th, 1918 to serve in Palestine at Ishmala on Garrison duty. His service number was 216829. He was demobilised Feb. 7th, 1919.

It is likely that he married Mary Daws in 1921: the record lists him as Joseph E Shipstone.

From the 1939 Register he was living on Main Street in Basford with Mary and working as a Builders Labourer.

He died 1979 09 20, at Cossall.

Arthur Wells is listed in the Roll of Honour book. However the names are so common that it was impossible to find definitive records both before and after the war about him. Neither he nor his family were resident in the village in the 1911 census. He must have been resident in either of the villages during the war for his service to be included in the Roll of Honour book.

He joined the Royal Army Service Corps, Motor Transport as a Private on Jan. 14th, 1915. He served in Egypt from April 4th, to Oct. 26th, 1915, being stationed at Alexandria and Cairo.   From then to 1919 he served in Salonika and was discharged on Mar. 27th, 1919.

An ailments form of 1915 describes a private A Wells, aged 23, service number 33710/30710, being admitted with nasal polyps on 1915 05 06. He was transferred to a sick convoy, was under observation for 16 days and aboard the hospital ship, Asturias. He was with the Army Service Corps. Motor Transport Battalion for five months, that time being with the field force..

There was no Woolcott family present in either of the villages in 1911. **Thomas Woolcott** (1886 11 17) whose military record is recorded in the Roll of Honour book, must subsequently have moved into either village. He may have lived in Far Cotton, Northants, in 1911, and boarded with the Yorke family. William Gregory Yorke, 58, was a blacksmith living with his wife and daughter, 21. A Thomas Woolcott, 24, also a blacksmith, from Hove in Sussex, boarded with him.

The Roll of Honour book describes him as joining the Royal Army Service Corps as a Shoeing Smith on Nov. 14th, 1914. His nearly five years of service is briefly described as serving four years in France and Belgium, and being stationed at Ypres and Jassy. He was demobilised on June 11th, 1919.

Further research found a Thomas Woolcott born c.1887 of 14, Woodsworth St., Hove, Sussex serving in the Army Service Corps with a Regimental Number, 4596.

The 1939 Register has a Thomas R Woolcott, living on Strelley Road, born 1886 11 17 and working at a colliery as miner below ground. His wife is listed simply as Ellen H.

Fig. 34 The wedding group photograph of James Faulconbridge in 1916

Photograph courtesy of John Blai

Epilogue

Each year the parishioners of Bilborough and Strelley gather around the Calvary in Strelley church graveyard that is the memorial to those who fell in the Great War. Alongside the memorial are military headstones of those who died of illness or immediately after the war of illness or injuries sustained during the war.

The village of Strelley has changed little over the past century. The graveyard is a little fuller, the medieval church has lost its pinnacles, the trees may be bigger or have died and been replaced. The M1 motorway passes through the valley just beyond the village, invisible, but for its sounds that appear like that of rushing water. It is believed that the planners intended the motorway to pass immediately to the south of the church and the historic 'motte' (the motte of a 'Norman motte and bailey') effectively cutting the village in two. The last of the squires, Mary Edge, a spinster, and by all accounts a 'femme formidable', had words with the planners and the motorway was routed around the village. The loop can be seen on maps. Currently the HS2 rail line is planned to pass just to the north of the church, albeit through a tunnel. It would appear that the speed of the train will not allow it to travel alongside the M1 round the loop and so it must follow a straight line taking it through the village.

If those remembered in the churchyard were to return they would probably recognise the place that they had left, although they would perhaps wonder what was creating the noise produced by the M1.

At the last memorial service on Nov. 11th all were gathered in the churchyard, each with their own thoughts during the two minutes silence. The day was clear and a few leaves still remained on the trees. The gentle breeze of the day dislodged a leaf and it drifted gently down to earth to join the many others that carpeted the grass. It seemed a symbol of the men honoured by the memorial, the few who fell among the many, but, who for us, had names and therefore we could share their tragedy and that of their families.

BIBLIOGRAPHY
Strelley & Bilborough: Great War Roll of Honour, D P Clifford   Moorleys Print and Publishing, www.moorleys.co.uk. ISBN 978 0 86071 703 4

1. How Our Ancestors Lived by David Hey. St. Edmunds Bury Press, Bury St. Edmunds, 2002. ISBN 1 903365 21X.

2. www.localhistories.org/life

3. 20th Century Britain. Economic, Social and Cultural Changes. Edited by Paul Johnson. Longman, London and New York,; 1994, page 112. ISBN 0 582 22817 4PPR.

4. The Long Trail. www.1914-1918.net/recruitment.htm

5. History of the Great War, Medical Sciences, General History, Edited by Major-General MacPherson, Vol.1, pages 134-135.
see www.vlib.us/medical/dentrecruit.htm

6a. Wikipedia. J P Edmonds, Military Operations: France and Belgium: 1916, vol. i (London 1932), page 152.

6b. Wikipedia. Statistics of the Military Effort of the British Empire during the Great War, 1914-1920 (London: 1922).

7. www.parliament.uk.

8. bbc.co.uk/schools/ww1

9. Wikipedia. Daily Telegraph, Thurs., 17 Feb., 1916.

10. Wikipedia. Froud R. Height, Health and History. Cambridge University press, 1996.

11. BBC News Magazine. 25th February, 2014. Article by Dan Snow.

12. British Historical Statistics by B P Mitchell.

13. www.wirksworth.org.uk. Information taken from the British Labour Statistics: Historical   Abstract 1886-1968. (Department of Employment and Productivity, 1971) and Brown and Hopkins, 1955.

General sources
Ancestry Library.com
Findmypast.com
Forces-war-records.co.uk

Appendix 1. List of all men: dates and places of birth and death

Surname	First Name	Born	Place of Birth	Died	Place of Death	Age in 1911	Resident in villages 1911
Allen	John William	1881 08 07	Lincs., Wilsford	1953 04 29	Notts.	30	Yes
Baines	Alfred James	1892 00 00	Notts., Newark			19	Yes
Barnes	William Panton	1876 02 04	Lincs., Stainfield	1944 06 24	Somerset, Frome	35	Yes
Beardsley	John Henry					30	Yes
Blatherwick	Charles Walter	1896 04 05	Leics., Old Darby	1978 03 00	Notts.	14	Yes
Blatherwick	George Thomas	1899 10 22	Leics., Old Darby	1964 03 00	Derbys., Belper	12	Yes
Booth	Joseph William	1895 04 11	Notts., Bilborough	1975 06 00	Cornwall, Falmouth	15	Yes
Booth	William Edward	1881 07 25	Notts., Lenton	1945 02 07	Notts., Nottm	29	Yes
Booth	Herbert	1899 11 26	Notts., Bilborough			11	Yes
Boyfield	James	1884 00 00	Rutland, Langham	1929 06 00	Northants, Kettering	26	Yes
Boyfield	Thomas	1877 4Q	Leics., Brooksby			33	Yes
Bradshaw	William	1874 05 27	Notts., Greasely	1955 03 00	Notts.	36	Yes
Breedon	Charles Edward	1867 10 00	Notts., Upton	1927 Q1		43	Yes
Burton	John	1870 00 00	Leics., Easton			41	Yes
Burton	John	1890 08 13	Notts., Bilborough	1955 03 29	Notts., Redhill	20	Yes
Burton	John Henry	1881 11 05	Notts., Bilborough	1959 1Q	Notts., Bingham	29	Yes
Burton	William	1900 00 00	Notts., Bilborough			11	Yes
Charlton	Albert	1889 06 20	Notts., Strelley	1955 06 24	Notts.	21	Yes
Charlton	Edgar	1892 07 15	Notts., Strelley	1968 12 00	Notts.	18	Yes
Cooper	Frederick	1876 00 00	Notts., Strelley			35	Yes
Davenport	Joseph	1882 00 00	Cheshire, Macclesfield	1967 03 00		28	Yes
Dawn	Herbert	1892 05 00	Notts., Witton	1941 09 00	London	18	Yes
Dean	John	1877 05 06	Notts., Annesley			38	Yes
Dunmore	John Thomas	1893 05 29	Lincs., West Deeping			19	Yes
Dunmore	Walter	1898 3Q	Lincs., Little Ponton	1978 09 00	Notts., Ilkeston	14	Yes
Dunmore	William	1901 12 08	Lincs., Little Ponton	1980 4Q	Derbys., Derby	10	Yes
Faulconbridge	Joseph	1867 00 00	Notts., Strelley	1935 09 00	Notts.	44	Yes
Faulconbridge	Thomas	1874 01 00	Notts., Beeston	1939 09 00	Notts.	37	Yes
Flack	James Henry	1888 07 00	London, Hatchern(end?)	1957 05 30	Sussex	22	Yes
Flack	Terrell	1864 07 03	Suffolk, Lakenheath	1945 06 00	Notts., Nottingham	43	Yes

Surname	First Name	Born	Place of Birth	Died	Place of Death	Age in 1911	Resident in villages 1911
Fletcher	Arthur	1875 00 00	Notts., Bilborough	1937 4Q	Notts	35	Yes
Frain	William	1883 00 00	Ireland			28	Yes
Frain	Tom	1889 00 00	Ireland, Kilmore			22	Yes
Goode	John	1893 07 14	Notts., Bunny			17	Yes
Goode	Harry	1900 01 08	Notts., Bilborough	1957 01 09	Notts., Bilsthorpe	11	Yes
Green	Charles Walter	1894 09 00	Derbys., Riddings	1980 3Q	Notts., Nottingham	16	Yes
Green	Fred	1893 00 00	Derbys., Riddings	1917 04 07	France	18	Yes
Green	Sam	1867 11 23	Notts., Mansfield	1925 07 28	Australia, Helensburgh	45	Yes
Hardy	William Ebenezer	1867 12 17	Notts., Kimberley	1941 02 21		43	Yes
Headland	Charles	1881 00 00	Lincs., Honington	1964 09 00	Notts.	30	Yes
Henson	George Henry	1887 07 26	Notts., Old Basford			23	Yes
Henson	Harold	1887 09 04	Notts., Kimberley	1970 12 00	Notts., Nottingham	23	Yes
Henson	Samuel Renny	1889 10 04	Notts., Kimberley	1980 03 00	Notts.	21	Yes
Henson	Thomas Cecil	1886 02 05	Notts., Kimberley	1952 12 11	Notts.	28	Yes
Hipwell	John (A)	1881 09 24	Derbys., Winshill	1914 3Q	Staffs., Burton	30	Yes
Housley	Joseph	1888 04 07	Notts., Greasely	1969 12 00	Notts.	22	Yes
Jackson	Tom	1869 00 00	Lincs., Beckingham	1957 00 00		42	Yes
Jackson	Hector	1900 03 13	Lincs., Easton	1978 09 09	Notts., Wollaton	11	Yes
Monks	William	1867 00 00	Notts., Strelley			44	Yes
Moore	William	1875 12 15	Notts., Carrington	1956 12 00	Notts., Nottingham	35	Yes
Moore	William Redvers	1900 04 14		1982 12 00		10	Yes
Morley	Samuel	1878 1Q	Notts., Kimberley	1925 03 00	Notts.	33	Yes
Murden	James	1878 00 00	Notts., Babbington	1943 03 00		33	Yes
Murden	Herbert	1886 10 25	Notts., Bilborough	1962 4Q	Notts., Bingham	24	Yes
Musgrove	John	1870 05 00	Notts., Strelley			40	Yes
Musgrove	John	1895 08 05	Notts., Toton			15	Yes
Neal	Frederick John	1884 00 00	Surrey, Wandsworth	1938 04 00	Notts., Newark	27	Yes
Oagelen	Thomas	1894 00 00	Notts., Nottingham			17	Yes
Oldershaw	John Harris	1892 07 00	Notts., Strelley	1965 11 25	Notts., Newark	18	Yes
Papworth	Albert Harold	1897 06 00	Hunts., Ramsey	1964 12 00	Notts., Nottingham	13	Yes
Payne	George Alfred	1867 00 00	Kent, Kennington			43	Yes
Phillip	John	1893 00 00	London			18	Yes
Pinchin	Edward	1867 00 00	Gloucs., Chedworth	1958 03 00		43	Yes

Surname	First Name	Born	Place of Birth	Died	Place of Death	Age In 1911	Resident In villages 1911
Porter	Fred	1882 1Q	Lincs., Swinstead			28	Yes
Powell	Arthur	1887 00 00	Wales, Monmouth			24	Yes
Rayner	Stanley	1890 08 19	Notts., Eastwood	1960 06 00	Leics., Leicester	20	Yes
Richards	John	1873 00 00	Notts., Kimberley	1956 2Q	Notts., Nottingham	38	Yes
Richards	Joseph	1882 00 00	Notts., Kimberley			28	Yes
Samways	Harry (S)	1890 00 00	Derbys., Norbury	1950 09 00	Derbys., Derby	19	Yes
Shaw	Robert Arthur Hillary	1898 07 31	Notts., Kimberley	1967 03 00	Notts., Southwell	12	Yes
Sibey	Sidney	1888 03 22	Lincs., Stapleford	1939 12 00	Notts.	23	Yes
Sibey	George Henry	1879 03 12	Lincs., Barsingham	1969 00 00	Yorks., Bradford	32	Yes
Simpkin	Edward	1870 00 00	Notts., Bilborough	1924 09 00	Notts., Nottingham	40	Yes
Sly	Frederick	1876 06 18	Notts., Strelley	1960 3Q	Notts.	34	Yes
Smith	James	1877 00 00	Notts., Bilborough	1957 00 00	Notts.	34	Yes
Smith	Harry	1899 00 00	Notts., Bilborough	1969 00 00	Notts.	12	Yes
Smith	Jesse Harry	1875 00 00	Beds., Cranfield	1925 06 00	Notts., Bingham	36	Yes
Smith	Harry	1894 00 00	Notts., Basford			17	Yes
Stevenson	Frank	1880 10 19	Notts., Strelley	1950 4Q		30	Yes
Stevenson	Samuel	1871 04 00	Notts., Strelley	1922 09 00	Notts.	39	Yes
Stevenson	Frank	1873 04 29	Notts., Strelley	1942 12 00		38	Yes
Taylor	Percy	1882 10 02	Derbys., Alderwasley	1958 06 00	Notts.	28	Yes
Thomson	Ernest Montague	1870 07 08	London	1960 02 25	Suffolk	41	Yes
Tuckwood	William	1888 03 29	Notts., Barton	1962 09 00	Notts., Nottingham	23	Yes
Underwood	Harry Herbert	1872 00 00	Northants, Maidford			38	Yes
Wagstaff	Harry	1885 04 10	Notts., Radford	1953 06 00		28	Yes
Wallbank	George	1890 02 12	Staffs., Bircheshead	1960 12 00	Warks, Birmingham	21	Yes
Wheatley	Albert	1884 01 00	Notts., Eastwood			27	Yes
Whitney	William	1880 02 22	Notts., Hucknall Torkard	1957 06 00	Notts., Southwell	30	Yes
Whitney	Henry	1884 10 30	Notts., Hucknall Torkard	1969 1Q	Notts., Newark	26	Yes
Wilkinson	Fred	1885 04 14	Lincs., N. Ormsby	1972 03 00	Lincs., Spalding	25	Yes
Wilson	James William	1893 08 19	Notts., Brough			17	Yes
Wilson	William	1892 00 00	Yorks., Reighton			19	Yes
Woodhouse	John	1880 3Q	Notts., Bilborough	1934 3Q	Notts., Nottingham	30	Yes
Woodhouse	Archibald Thomas	1886 07 17	Notts., Bilborough	1970 06 00	Notts., Nottingham	24	Yes
Wright	William	1883 08 26	Lincs., Donnington	1958 02 26		27	Yes

Surname	First Name	Born	Place of Birth	Died	Place of Death	Age in 1911	Resident in villages 1911
Appleyard	George	1898 2Q	Lincs., Carrington	1950 2Q	Notts., Nottingham	12	No
Appleyard	Henry	1900 09 00	Lincs., Carrington			10	No
Booth	John Henry	1897 10 29	Notts., Bilborough	1983 09 00	Notts., Nottingham	13	Yes
Brewster	Edwin George	1895 09 17	Notts., Bilborough	1918 09 20	France	15	Yes
Brewster	Wilfred Charles	1898 12 24	Notts., Strelley	1935 00 00	Notts., Mansfield	12	Yes
Brewster	William John	1897 08 28	Notts., Strelley	1959 11 09	Notts.	13	Yes
Carlisle	Frederick	1896 09 16	Notts., Bilborough			14	Yes
Dale	Cyril	1891 11 26	Notts., Newark	1981 12 00	Notts.	19	No
Dobney	George	1897 00 00	Lincs., Gosberton	1918 08 29	France	13	No
Edge	Ralph Thomas	1888 09 23	Notts., Southwell	1972 09 00	Sussex, Midhurst	22	Yes
Edge	James Vernon	1889 10 12	Notts., Southwell	1971 06 00	Cumberland, Cockermouth	21	No
Edge	Roger Francis	1897 10 15	Notts., Strelley	1984 05 00	Sussex, Hayward's Heath	13	No
Faulconbridge	James	1890 11 19	Notts., Radford	1969 02 00	Notts.	20	Yes
Flack	George	1892 01 20	Norfolk, Weeting	1958 01 24	Notts.	19	Yes
Flack	William	1896 00 00	Norfolk, Weeting	1915 12 02	Gallipoli	15	Yes
Garton	Ferdinand	1884 09 24	Notts., Kimberley	1962 3Q	Notts.	27	No
Goode	Alvin	1892 11 11	Notts., Bunny	1940 03 00	Notts., Nottingham	20	No
Goode	Thomas	1889 09 16	Notts., Ruddington	1954 2Q	Notts.	21	Yes
Goode	William	1894 09 15	Notts., Bunny			18	Yes
Greenham	George	1883 00 00	Notts., Hyson Green	1925 3Q	Notts., Nottingham	28	Yes
Henson	Sidney Scott	1896 10 00	Notts., Trowell	1942 1Q	Derbys., Ilkeston	14	Yes
Henson	Charles Wilfred	1892 01 00	Notts., Trowell	1918 08 20	Suffolk, Ipswich (Strelley?)	19	Yes
Hudson	Edmund	1894 00 00	Yorks., Doncaster	1919 11 24	Notts., Strelley	16	No
Hudson	Robert Atkinson	1889 00 00	Westmorland, Longsleddale			22	No
Hudson	William	1887 00 00	Westmorland, Longsleddale			24	No
Hughes	Harry Alfred	1879 00 00	Staffs., Wolver'ton	1920 06 17	Notts., Strelley	31	Yes
Jackson	Herbert	1897 00 00	Lincs., Easton			14	No
Mann	Cornelius	1892 11 07	Norfolk, New Houghton			18	Yes
Mellor	William Street	1881 02 16	Derbys., Ilkeston			30	Yes
Moore	Albert	1892 00 00	Notts., Carrington			19	Yes
Moore	Thomas	1888 05 21	Notts., Carrington			22	No
Palin	Alfred John	1895 00 00	Notts., Strelley	1916 05 23	France	16	Yes
Pearson	Thomas William	1900 06 02	Notts., Nottingham	1974 12 29	Notts., Rushcliffe	11	No

Surname	First Name	Born	Place of Birth	Died	Place of Death	Age in 1911	Resident villages 1911
Pinchin	James Edward	1896 05 13	Worcs., Upper Hawley	1974 10 06	Notts.	14	Yes
Raynor	Joseph Frederick	1889 11 19	Notts., Strelley	1949 1Q	Notts.	21	Yes
Shipstone	Joseph Ewart	1898 05 19	Notts., Bulwell	1979 09 20	Notts., Cossall	14	No
Stevenson	Simeon	1898 01 01	Notts., Kimberley	1959 1Q	Notts.	13	Yes
Wells	Arthur	1891 00 00				21	No
Woodhouse	Joseph	1880 10 25	Notts., Strelley	1972 2Q		30	Yes
Woolcott	Thomas	1887 00 00	Northants., Far Cotton			15	No

Appendix 2. Age, regiment, marital status and occupations

Surname	First Name	Age 1911	Regiment	Marital Status	Occupation
Dunmore	William	9		Single	
Appleyard	Henry	10	Royal Navy	Single	
Moore	William Redvers	10	Labour Corps	Gwendoline M ?	Farmer & Threshing machine driver
Booth	Herbert	11		Single	Farm worker
Burton	William	11		Olive Archer (1933)	Farm worker
Goode	Harry	11		Lois Cartledge (1919)	Coal merchant
Jackson	Hector	11		Ada Robinson (1925)	Milk retailer
Pearson	Thomas William	11	Royal Air Force	Frances M Allen (1930)	Farm worker
Appleyard	George	12	Sherwood Foresters	Eliza Caulton (1919)	Farm worker
Blatherwick	Gerorge Thomas	12		Maggie Coleman (1920)	Foreman Road Construction
Brewster	Wilfred Charles	12	Royal Garrison Artillery	Gertrude G Greaves (1929)	Miner
Shaw	Robert Arthur H	12		Elizabeth Wilson (1924)	Farmer
Smith	Harry	12	Sherwood Foresters	Mary Gwendoline Ruth Nash (1921)	Miner
Booth	John Henry	13	Royal Field Artillery	Ethel Pinchin (1929)	Farm worker
Brewster	William John	13	Royal Field Artillery	Alice M Smith (1929)	Miner, Pot. & Fish Fryer Shop Keeper
Dobney	George	13	South Notts. Hussars	Single	Merchant
Edge	Roger Francis	13	Coldstream Guards	Single	Farm worker
Papworth	Albert Harold	13		Florence M P Wayman (1931)	Miner
Stevenson	Simeon	13	Coldstream Guards	Elizabeth A Holmes (1925)	Miner
Blatherwick	Charles Walter	14		Lily M Randall (1922)	Farm worker
Carlisle	Frederick	14	Royal Flying Corps	Single	Apprentice Engineer
Dunmore	Walter	14	Sherwood Foresters		Farm worker
Green	George E	14		Edith A ? (?)	Miner
Henson	Sidney Scott	14	South Notts Hussars	Sarah E Everitt (1924)	Farmer (poultry)
Jackson	Herbert	14	Royal Field Artillery	Single	Groom
Pinchin	James Edward	14	Royal Air Force	Single	Apprentice fitter
Shipstone	Joseph Ewart	14	Royal Garrison Artillery	Mary Daws (1921)	Labourer
Booth	Joseph William	15	Canadian Overseas Exped'y Force		Tobacco machinist

Surname	First Name	Age 1911	Regiment	Marital Status	Occupation
Brewster	**Edwin George**	**15**	**Royal Field Artillery**	**Single**	**Gardener, domestic**
Flack	**William**	**15**	**Royal Field Artillery**	**Single**	**Milk delivery boy**
Musgrove	John	15		Eliza A Kightley (1920)	Servant, Farm worker
Green	Charles Walter	16	Sherwood Foresters	Single	Miner
Hudson	**Edmund**	**16**	**London Scottish 14th Batt.**	**Single**	**Clerk, railway**
Palin	**Alfred John**	**16**	**Royal Field Artillery**	**Single**	**Miner**
Goode	John	17	Sherwood Foresters	Mary Ellen ?	Miner
Oagelen	Thomas	17		Single	Farm worker
Smith	Harry	17		Single	Blacksmith
Wilson	James William	17	Royal Engineers	Single (also in 1917)	Farm worker
Charlton	Edgar	18	Labour Corps	Alice H Everitt (1931)	Locomotive fireman
Dawn	Herbert	18	**Royal Field Artillery**	Single	Farm, Waggoner
Goode	**William**	**18**	**Royal Field Artillery**	**Single**	Footman, Valet
Green	Fred	18		Ada Ann Osborne (1918)	**Groom. Miner. Labourer**
Mann	**Cornelius**	**18**	**Royal Army Service Corps**	**Leah Taylor (1919)**	**Farmer, poultry**
Oldershaw	John Harris	18	Royal Field Artillery	Mary A Hilton (1916)	Clerk, assistant poor law
Phillip	John	18	Royal Fusiliers	Single	Farm worker
Baines	Alfred James	19	**Royal Horse Artillery**	Elizabeth Beck (1932)	Groom
Dale	**Cyril**	**19**	Royal Field Artillery	**Winifred Ward (1924)**	**Groom**
Dunmore	John Thomas	19	**Royal Army Medical Corps**	Single	Farm worker
Flack	**George**	**19**		**Dorothy S Veal (1923)**	**Tobacco machine foreman**
Henson	**Charles Wilfred**	**19**	**Sherwood Foresters**	**Annie Jukes (1916)**	**Miner**
Moore	**Albert**	**19**	**Sherwood Foresters**	**Single**	**Apprentice, Electrical Engineering**
Samways	Harry (S)	19	Royal Field Artillery	Single	Servant, odd job man
Wilson	William	19		Single	Groom
Burton	John	20		Single	Apprentice electrician
Faulconbridge	**James**	**20**	**Sherwood Foresters**	**Agnes Skerry (1916)**	**Miner, engineman**
Goode	**Alvin**	**20**	**Sherwood Foresters**	**Gladys E Burden (1920)**	**Farm worker. Miner**
Rayner	Stanley	20	Royal Army Service Corps	Eleanor Wright (1913)	Railway Shunter, signalman
Charlton	Albert	21		Florence Mills (1915)	Farm Waggoner

Surname	First Name	Age 1911	Regiment	Marital Status	Occupation
Edge	**James Vernon**	**21**	**Sherwood Foresters**	**Rachel M Young (1921)**	**Farm & Chartered Land Agent**
Goode	**Thomas**	**21**	Sherwood Foresters	Jane ?	Farm worker
Henson	Samuel Renny	21	Sherwood Foresters	Fanny Stevenson (1915)	Miner. Farmer
Raynor	**Joseph Frederick**	**21**	Sherwood Foresters	**Margaret Wood (1918)**	**Miner. Shop keeper, general grocer**
Wallbank	George (Wilfred)	21	West Riding	S ???? (????)	Gardener. Upholsterer
Wells	**Arthur**	**21**	**Royal Army Service Corps**	**Single**	
Edge	**Ralph Thomas**	**22**	**Royal Engineers**	**Gladys Marr Torr (1919)**	**Civil Engineer**
Flack	James Henry	22	Surrey Regiment	Margaret E Warnes (1944)	
Frain	Tom	22		Florence Toplis (1913)	Farm worker
Housley	Joseph	22		Single	Miner
Hudson	**Robert Atkinson**	**22**	**Sherwood Foresters**	**Single**	**Farm horseman**
Moore	**Thomas**	**22**	**Royal Army Service Corps**		
Henson	George Henry	23	Sherwood Foresters	Lily B Hopewell (1911)	Miner
Henson	Harold	23		Sabina Johnson (1914)	Miner. Farmer
Sibey	Sidney	23	Royal Army Service Corps	Brenda Victoria Charlton (1912)	Blacksmith, colliery
Tuckwood	William	23		Single in 1939	Farm worker
Hudson	**William**	**24**	**Lincolnshire Regiment**	**Single**	**Farm worker**
Murden	Herbert	24		Maria Dawson (1914)	Miner. Billiard Room Attendant
Powell	Arthur	24	Royal Army Service Corps	Single	Gardener
Woodhouse	Archibald Thomas	24		Muriel H Kirk (1923)	Miner. Tobacco worker
Woolcott	**Thomas**	**24**	**Royal Army Service Corps**	**Ellen H ?**	**Shoeing Smith. Miner**
Wilkinson	Fred	25		Mary Ann Cook (1917)	Chauffeur
Boyfield	James	26	Royal Army Service Corps	Alice K Headland (1921)	Farm, waggoner
Whitney	Henry	26		Annie Tunstall (1908)	Farmer, Haulage contractor
Garton	**Ferdinand**	**27**	**Royal Marine Light Infantry**	**Lily Stenson (1937)**	**Miner**
Neal	Frederick John	27		Single	Butler
Wheatley	Albert	27		Lois Johnson (1907)	Miner
Wright	William	27		Tilley ? (?)	Waggoner on farm Timber haulier

Surname	First Name	Age 1911	Regiment	Marital Status	Occupation
Davenport	Joseph	28		Annie ? (1910)	Groom
Frain	William	28			Farm worker
Greenham	**George**	**28**	**Sherwood Foresters**	**Ann Dobney (1910)**	**Woodman**
Henson	Thomas Cecil	28		Mary Ellen Johnson (1912)	Miner. Dairy farmer
Porter	Fred	28	Sherwood Foresters	Isobelle ? (1908)	Shepherd
Richards	Joseph	28		Lottie Beadman (1915)	Miner
Taylor	Percy	28		Mary Attenborough (1903)	Haulage contractor
Wagstaff	Harry	28		Mary Ann Swaby (1908)	Tobacco Blender
Booth	William Edward	29		Margaret MacRae (1910)	Blacksmith, colliery
Burton	John Henry	29		Lily Hagues (1904)	Farmer
Allen	John William	30	Training Reserve	Kate Tunnard (1906)	Commercial Traveller Breweries
Beardsley	John Henry	30		Lily Ann Walton (1909)	Farm, waggoner
Headland	Charles	30			Gardener & gen. lab.
Hipwell	John (A)	30	Royal Field Artillery/RGA	Mary Ann Bloor (1908)	Farm worker
Mellor	**William Street**	**30**	**Royal Naval Voluntary Reserve**	**Ellen Roberts (1908)**	**Teacher, Elementary School**
Stevenson	Frank	30	Sherwood Foresters	Florence A Burton (1914)	Engineers fitter
Whitney	William	30		Betty M Hardin (1919)	Farmer
Woodhouse	John	30		Elizabeth Beardsley (1919)	Farm worker
Woodhouse	**Joseph**	**30**	**South Notts. Hussars**	**Edith ? (1910)**	**Farmer (son of)**
Hughes	**Harry Alfred**	**31**	**Royal Army Ordinance Corps**	**Mary Ann or Margaret (1909)**	**Insurance agent**
Sibey	George Henry	32	Sherwood Foresters	Edith Annie ? (1907)	Blacksmith. Agricultural Engineer
Boyfield	Thomas	33		Single	Farm, waggoner
Morley	Samuel	33	Sherwood Foresters	Ada Barker (1909)	Insurance agent
Murden	James	33		Mabel ? (1907)	Miner
Sly	Frederick	34	Sherwood Foresters	Eliza J Smith (1921)	Carter for colliery
Smith	James	34	Sherwood Foresters	Elizabeth Stevenson (1898)	Carter at colliery
Barnes	William Panton	35	RAF	Henrietta Maidment (1900)	Gardener, domestic
Cooper	Frederick	35		Mary Ann Harris (1897)	Miner
Fletcher	Arthur	35		Mary Ann Smith (1900)	Miner

Surname	First Name	Age 1911	Regiment	Marital Status	Occupation
Moore	William	35	Sherwood Foresters	Elizabeth Elkington (1899)	Farmer
Bradshaw	William	36		Sarah Elizabeth Severn (1904)	Miner and Grazier
Smith	Jesse Harry	36		Fanny Hammond (1893)	Farm worker
Faulconbridge	Thomas	37		Betsy May ? (1900)	Miner, static engine drive-
Dean	John	38		Clara Stevenson (1905)	Roadman (Council), Miner
Richards	John	38		Single	Miner
Stevenson	Frank	38		Alice Soar (1897)	Miner
Underwood	Harry Herbert	38		Lizzie Harris (1896)	Game keeper
Stevenson	Samuel	39		Single	Miner
Musgrove	John	40		Ellen ? (1893)	Miner
Simpkin	Edward	40	Sherwood Foresters	Mary ? (1902)	Farm worker
Burton	John	41		Alice Blatherwick (1898)	Farm worker
Thomson	Ernest Montague	41	Chaplain	Louisa Daniel 1901 07 09	Clerk in holy orders
Jackson	Tom	42		Emma Roberts (1895)	Traction Engine Driver
Breedon	Charles Edward	43		Kate Elizabeth Barlow (1892)	Chauffeur
Flack	Terrell	43		Martha Maria Malt (1887)	Gamekeeper
Hardy	William Ebenezer	43		Dorothea Kate ? (1910)	Brewer
Payne	George Alfred	43		Cordelia ? (1902)	Public House Manager
Pinchin	Edward	43		Louisa Clarke (1895)	Farm worker
Faulconbridge	Joseph	44		Henrietta Grainger (1890)	Colliery Stoker
Monks	William	44		Emma Alice Ryder (1891)	Farmer
Green	Sam	45		Eliza Ann Dickinson (1892)	Farm worker

Surnames in bold are those of the men in the 'Roll of Honour' book.
The spouse is named regardless of the date the couple were married.
The marital status, single, is that stated in the census of 1911, if no details of marriage could be found.

Appendix 3. Date and places of birth and death, and age in 1911.

Surname	First Name	Date of birth	Place Birth	Date of death	Place Died	Age in 1911	Resident in 1911
Wallbank	George (Wilfred)	1890 02 12	Staffs., Bircheshead	1960 12 00	Warks, Birmingham	21	Yes
Booth	William Edward	1881 07 25	Notts., Lenton	1945 02 07	Notts., Nottm	29	B
Flack	James Henry	1888 07 00	London, Hatchern(end?)	1957 05 30	Sussex	22	B
Dobney	George	1897 00 00	Lincs., Gosberton Risegate	1918 08 29	France	13	No
Henson	Sidney Scott	1896 10 00	Notts., Trowell	1942 1Q	Derbys., Ilkeston	14	S
Woodhouse	Joseph	1880 10 25	Notts., Strelley	1972 2Q		30	B
Appleyard	George	1898 2Q	Lincs., Carrington	1960 2Q	Notts., Nottingham	12	No
Edge	James Vernon	1889 10 12	Notts., Southwell	1971 06 00	Cumberland, Cockermouth	21	No
Greenham	George	1883 00 00	Notts., Hyson Green	1925 3Q	Notts., Nottingham	28	B
Henson	Charles Wilfred	1892 01 00	Notts., Trowell	1918 08 20	Suffolk, Ipswich	19	S
Moore	Albert	1892 00 00	Notts., Carrington			19	B
Hudson	Robert Atkinson	1889 00 00	Westmorland, Longsleddale			22	No
Raynor	Joseph Frederick	1889 11 19	Notts., Strelley	1949 1Q	Notts.	21	S
Goode	Alvin	1892 11 11	Notts., Bunny	1940 03 00	Notts., Nottingham	20	No
Faulconbridge	James	1890 11 19	Notts., Radford	1969 12 00	Notts.	20	S
Simpkin	Edward	1870 00 00	Notts., Bilborough	1924 09 00	Notts., Nottingham	40	S
Moore	William	1875 12 15	Notts., Carrington	1956 12 00	Notts., Nottingham	35	B
Sly	Frederick	1876 06 18	Notts., Strelley	1960 3Q	Notts.	34	S
Smith	James	1877 00 00	Notts., Bilborough	1957 00 00		34	S
Morley	Samuel	1878 1Q	Notts., Kimberley	1925 03 00		33	S
Sibey	George Henry	1879 03 12	Lincs., Barsingham	1969 00 00	Yorks., Bradford	32	B
Stevenson	Frank	1880 10 19	Notts., Strelley	1950 4Q		30	B
Porter	Fred	1882 1Q	Lincs., Swinstead			28	S
Henson	George Henry	1887 07 26	Notts., Old Basford			23	B
Goode	Thomas	1889 09 16	Notts., Ruddington	1954 2Q	Notts.	21	B
Goode	John	1893 07 14	Notts., Bunny	1957 01 09	Notts., Bilsthorpe	17	B
Green	Charles Walter	1894 09 00	Derbys., Riddings	1917 04 07	France	16	S
Dunmore	Walter	1898 3Q	Lincs., Little Ponton	1978 09 00	Notts., Ilkeston	14	S
Smith	Harry	1899 00 00	Notts., Bilborough	1969 00 00	Notts.	12	S

Surname	First Name	Date of birth	Place Birth	Date of death	Place Died	Age in 1911	Resident in 1911
Thomson	Ernest Montague	1870 07 08	London	1960 02 25	Suffolk	41	B
Appleyard	Henry	1900 09 00	Lincs., Carrington			10	No
Mellor	William Street	1881 02 16	Derbys., Ilkeston			30	B
Garton	Ferdinand	1884 09 24	Notts., Kimberley	1962 3Q		27	No
Dale	Cyril	1891 11 26	Notts., Newark	1981 12 00	Notts.	19	No
Shipstone	Joseph Ewart	1898 05 19	Notts., Bulwell	1979 09 20	Notts., Cossall	14	B
Brewster	Wilfred Charles	1898 12 24	Notts., Strelley	1935 00 00	Notts., Mansfield	12	B
Baines	Alfred James	1892 00 00	Notts., Newark			19	B
Carlisle	Frederick	1896 09 16	Notts., Bilborough			14	B
Headland	Charles	1881 00 00	Lincs., Honington	1964 09 00	Notts.	30	S
Brewster	Edwin George	1895 09 17	Notts., Bilborough	1918 09 20	France	15	B
Palin	Alfred John	1895 00 00	Notts., Strelley	1916 05 23	France	16	S
Jackson	Herbert	1897 00 00	Lincs., Easton			14	B
Samways	Harry (S)	1890 00 00	Derbys., Norbury	1950 09 00	Derbys., Derby	19	S
Dunmore	John Thomas	1893 05 29	Lincs., West Deeping			19	S
Phillip	John	1893 00 00	London			18	B
Goode	William	1894 09 15	Notts., Bunny			16	No
Flack	William	1896 00 00	Norfolk, Weeting	1915 12 02	Gallipoli	15	B
Booth	John Henry	1897 10 29	Notts., Bilborough	1983 09 00	Notts., Nottingham	13	B
Brewster	William John	1897 08 28	Notts., Strelley	1959 11 09	Notts.	13	B
Edge	Ralph Thomas	1888 09 23	Notts., Southwell	1972 09 00	Sussex, Midhurst	22	S
Wilson	James William	1893 08 19	Notts., Brough			17	B
Moore	Thomas	1888 05 21	Notts., Carrington			22	No
Boyfield	James	1884 00 00	Rutland, Langham	1929 06 00	Northants., Kettering	26	B
Powell	Arthur	1887 00 00	Wales, Monmouth			24	S
Sibey	Sidney	1888 03 22	Lincs., Stapleford	1939 12 00	Notts.	23	B
Wells	Arthur	1891 00 00				21	No
Rayner	Stanley	1890 08 19	Notts., Eastwood	1960 06 00	Leics., Leicester	20	B
Mann	Cornelius	1892 11 07	Norfolk, New Houghton			18	No
Woolcott	Thomas	1887 00 00	Northants., Far Cotton			15	No
Hughes	Harry Alfred	1879 00 00	Staffs., Wolverhampton	1920 06 17	Notts., Strelley	31	B
Flack	George	1892 01 20	Norfolk, Weeting	1958 01 24	Notts.	19	B
Pinchin	James Edward	1896 05 13	Worcs., Upper Hawley	1974 10 06	Notts.	14	B

Surname	First Name	Date of birth	Place Birth	Date of death	Place Died	Age in 1911	Resident in 1911
Pearson	**Thomas William**	**1900 06 02**	**Notts., Nottingham**	**1974 12 29**	**Notts., Rushcliffe**	**11**	**No**
Barnes	William Panton	1876 02 04	Lincs., Stainfield	1944 06 24	Somerset, Frome	35	S
Hudson	**Edmund**	**1894 00 00**	**Yorks., Doncaster**	**1919 11 24**	**Notts., Strelley**	**16**	**No**
Hudson	**William**	**1887 00 00**	**Westmorland, Longsleddale**			**24**	**No**
Moore	William Redvers	1900 04 14	Notts., Bilborough	1982 12 00	Notts., Nottingham	10	B
Dawn	Herbert	1892 05 00	Notts., Witton	1941 09 00	London	18	S
Edge	**Roger Francis**	**1897 10 15**	**Notts., Strelley**	**1984 05 00**	**Sussex, Hayward's Heath**	**13**	**No**
Stevenson	**Simeon**	**1898 01 01**	**Notts., Kimberley**	**1959 1Q**	**Notts.**	**13**	**S**
Booth	Joseph William	1895 04 11	Notts., Bilborough	1975 06 00	Cornwall, Falmouth	15	B
Faulconbridge	Joseph	1867 00 00	Notts., Strelley	1935 09 00	Notts.	44	S
Monks	William	1867 00 00	Notts., Strelley			44	S
Breedon	Charles Edward	1867 10 00	Notts., Upton	1927 1Q		43	B
Pinchin	Edward	1867 00 00	Gloucs., Chedworth	1958 03 00		43	B
Payne	George Alfred	1867 00 00	Kent, Kennington			43	B
Flack	Terrell	1864 07 03	Suffolk, Lakenheath	1945 06 00	Notts., Nottingham	43	S
Hardy	William Ebenezer	1867 12 17	Notts., Kimberley			43	B
Jackson	Tom	1869 00 00	Lincs., Beckingham	1957 00 00		42	B
Burton	John	1870 00 00	Leics., Easton			41	S
Musgrove	John	1870 05 00	Notts., Strelley			40	B
Stevenson	Samuel	1871 04 00	Notts., Strelley	1922 09 00	Notts.	39	S
Stevenson	Frank	1873 04 29	Notts., Strelley	1942 12 00		38	S
Underwood	Harry Herbert	1872 00 00	Northants., Maidford			38	B
Dean	John	1877 05 06	Notts., Annesley			38	B
Richards	John	1873 00 00	Notts., Kimberley	1956 2Q	Notts., Nottingham	38	B
Faulconbridge	Thomas	1874 01 00	Notts., Beeston	1939 09 00	Notts.	37	B
Smith	Jesse Harry	1875 00 00	Beds., Cranfield	1925 06 00	Notts., Bingham	36	S
Bradshaw	William	1874 05 27	Notts., Greasley	1955 03 00	Notts.	36	B
Fletcher	Arthur	1875 00 00	Notts., Bilborough	1937 4Q	Notts.	35	B
Cooper	Frederick	1876 00 00	Notts., Strelley			35	S
Murden	James	1878 00 00	Notts., Babbington	1943 03 00		33	B
Boyfield	Thomas	1877 4Q	Leics., Brooksby			33	B
Woodhouse	John	1880 3Q	Notts., Bilborough	1934 3Q	Notts., Nottingham	30	B
Hipwell	John (A)	1881 09 24	Derbys., Winshill	1914 3Q	Staffs., Burton	30	B

Surname	First Name	Date of birth	Place Birth	Date of death	Place Died	Age in 1911	Resident in 1911
Beardsley	John Henry	1881 08 07	Lincs., Wilsford	1953 04 29	Notts.	30	S
Allen	John William	1880 02 22	Notts., Hucknall Torkard	1957 06 00	Notts., Southwell	30	B
Whitney	William	1881 11 05	Notts., Bilborough	1959 1Q	Notts., Bingham	30	S
Burton	John Henry	1882 00 00	Cheshire, Macclesfield	1967 03 00		29	B
Davenport	Joseph	1882 00 00	Notts., Kimberley			28	S
Richards	Joseph	1882 10 02	Derbys., Alderwasley	1958 06 00	Notts.	28	B
Taylor	Percy	1886 02 05	Notts., Kimberley	1952 12 11	Notts.	28	B
Henson	Thomas Cecil	1883 00 00	Ireland			28	S
Frain	William	1884 01 00	Notts., Eastwood			27	B
Wheatley	Albert	1883 08 26	Surrey, Wandsworth	1958 02 26		27	S
Neal	Frederick John	1884 10 30	Lincs., Donnington	1969 1Q	Notts., Newark	27	S
Wright	William	1885 04 14	Notts., Hucknall Torkard	1972 03 00	Lincs., Spalding	26	B
Whitney	Henry	1885 04 10	Lincs., N. Ormsby	1953 06 00		25	B
Wilkinson	Fred	1886 07 17	Notts., Radford	1970 06 00	Notts., Nottingham	25	B
Wagstaff	Harry	1886 10 25	Notts., Bilborough	1962 4Q	Notts., Bingham	24	B
Woodhouse	Archibald Thomas	1887 09 04	Notts., Bilborough	1970 12 00	Notts., Nottingham	24	B
Murden	Herbert	1888 03 29	Notts., Kimberley	1962 09 00	Notts., Nottingham	23	B
Henson	Harold	1888 04 07	Notts., Barton	1969 12 00	Notts.	23	S
Tuckwood	William	1889 06 20	Notts., Greasley			22	B
Housley	Joseph		Ireland, Kilmore			22	S
Frain	Tom	1889 06 20	Notts., Strelley	1955 06 24	Notts.	21	B
Charlton	Albert	1889 10 04	Notts., Kimberley	1980 03 00	Notts.	21	S
Henson	Samuel Renny	1890 08 13	Notts., Bilborough	1955 03 29	Notts., Redhill	20	S
Burton	John	1892 00 00	Yorks., Reighton			19	B
Wilson	William	1892 07 15	Notts., Strelley	1968 12 00	Notts.	18	S
Charlton	Edgar	1893 00 00	Derbys., Riddings			18	S
Green	Fred	1892 07 00	Notts., Strelley	1925 07 28	Australia, Helensburgh	18	S
Oldershaw	John Harris	1894 00 00	Notts., Basford	1965 11 25	Notts., Newark	17	S
Smith	Harry	1894 00 00	Notts., Nottingham			17	B
Oagelen	Thomas	1895 08 05	Notts., Toton			15	S
Musgrove	John	1896 04 05	Leics., Old Darby	1988 04 00	Notts., Newark	14	Yes
Blatherwick	Charles Walter	1897 07 17	Derbys., Riddings	1978 03 00	Notts.	14	S
Green	George E			1989 05 00	Notts., Warsop		S

Surname	First Name	Date of birth	Place Birth	Date of death	Place Died	Age in 1911	Resident in 1911
Papworth	Albert Harold	1897 06 00	Hunts., Ramsey	1964 12 00	Notts., Nottingham	13	B
Blatherwick	George Thomas	1899 10 22	Leics., Old Darby	1964 03 00	Derbys., Belper	12	S
Shaw	Robert Arthur Hillary	1898 07 31	Notts., Kimberley	1967 03 00	Notts., Southwell	12	S
Goode	Harry	1900 01 08	Notts., Bilborough	1980 3Q	Notts., Nottingham	11	B
Jackson	Hector	1900 03 13	Lincs., Easton	1978 09 09	Notts., Wollaton	11	B
Booth	Herbert	1899 11 26	Notts., Bilborough			11	B
Burton	William	1900 00 00	Notts., Bilborough			11	B
Dunmore	William	1901 12 08	Lincs., Little Ponton	1980 4Q	Derbys., Derby	10	S

S = Strelley, B= Bilborough
Surnames in bold are those of the men in the 'Roll of Honour' book.

Appendix 4. Accommodation details of all males in the villages in 1911

Surname	First names	Marital Status	Age	Couple	Adult M	Adult F	Children M	Children F	Total	Number Rooms
Booth	Ronald Edward	S	0	1			1		3	5
Murden	Harry	S	0.08	1			1	2	5	5
Taylor	Horace Stevenson	S	0.33	1			1	2	5	3
Woodhouse	Cyril	S	0.5	1			1		3	4
Burton	William	S	1	1	1		2	1	6	10
Dean	Sydney	S	1	1	1		2	1	6	4
Dickson	Sydney	S	1	2	1		2	1	8	
Green	Sam	S	1	1	1		5	2	10	5
Walter (Walker?)	William Rowland	S	2	2		3	1	1	9	7
Cross	James	S	2		3	1	1		5	5
Burton	John Henry	S	3	1	1		2	1	6	10
Blatherwick	Albert	S	3	1	2		2	3	9	6
Dickman	Claude B	S	3	2			4		8	9
Bradshaw	Auburn	S	3	1			2	1	5	5
Faulconbridge	Harold	S	4	1			2	1	5	5
Dean	John	S	4	1	1		2	1	6	4
Faulconbridge	Thomas	S	5	1			2	1	5	5
Eley	Harold Edward	S	5	1			3	1	6	3
Simpkin	Edward Martin	S	5	1			3		5	3
Paling	Herbert James	S	6	1		2	1	2	6	6
Booth	Edward	S	6	1	4	3		1	11	5
Burton	Eric	S	6	1	2	1			7	5
Bradshaw	Cecil	S	7	1				2	5	5
Papworth	Redvers Reginald	S	7	1			2		4	4
Wilson	Thomas Edward	S	7	1			2	1	5	4
Fletcher	Arthur	S	7	1		1	1	2	6	3
Eley	George William	S	7	1			3	1	6	3
Blatherwick	William	S	7	1			4	3	9	6
Stevenson	Frank Robert	S	7	1			2		4	4

(Adult M, Adult F, Children M and Children F columns fall under the "Household" heading.)

Surname	First names	Marital Status	Age	Couple	Household Adult M	Adult F	Children M	Children F	Total	Number Rooms
Green	Percy L	S	7	1	1		5	2	10	5
Smith	Mark	S	7	1			3	1	6	4
Brewster	Thomas	S	8			1	3	2	6	6
Eley	Frank Wilton	S	8	1			3	1	6	3
Moore	Leslie George	S	8	1			2	3	7	8
Musgrove	Ned	S	9	1			1	3	6	3
Barnes	William Panton	S	9	1			1		3	5
Moore	**William Redvers**	**S**	**10**				2	3	7	8
Green	Tom D	S	10	1	1		5	2	10	5
Smith	James	S	10	1			3	1	6	4
Dunmore	William	S	10	1	1		1	2	6	5
Goode	Harry	S	11	1			3	1	6	5
Booth	Herbert	S	11	1	1	3	4	1	11	5
Jackson	Hector	S	11	1			2	2	6	5
Burton	William	S	11	1	2		2		7	5
Brewster	**Wilfred**	**S**	**12**			1	3	2	6	6
Blatherwick	George Thomas	S	12	1			4	3	9	6
Shaw	Robert Arthur Hillary	S	12	1		1	1		3	6
Smith	**Harry**	**S**	**12**	1			3	1	6	4
Papworth	Albert Harold	S	13			1	2	1	4	4
Brewster	**William**	**S**	**13**	1	1		3	1	6	5
Booth	**John Henry**	**S**	**13**	1	1	3	4	1	11	5
Stevenson	**Simeon**	**S**	**13**	1			2	1	4	4
Pinchin	**James**	**S**	**14**	1		1	1	2	6	6
Carlyle	**Fred**	**S**	**14**	1	1	2	1		4	5
Jackson	**Herbert**	**S**	**14**	1		2	2		6	5
Dunmore	**Walter**	**S**	**14**	1	1		1		2	6
Blatherwick	Charles Walter	S	14				4	3	9	6
Henson	**Sydney Scott**	**S**	**14**	1	4	1	1		7	6
Green	George E	S	14	1	1		5	2	10	5
Green	**George**	**S**	**15**			1	3	2	6	6
Booth	**Joseph William**	**S**	**15**	1	1	3	4	1	11	5

94

Surname	First names	Marital Status	Age	Couple	Adult M	Adult F	Children M	Children F	Total	Number Rooms
Flack	William Richard	S	15	1	3		1	1	7	5
Goode	William	S	16	1	3			1	6	5
Paling	Alfred John	S	16	1		2		2	6	6
Green	Charles Walter	S	16	1	1		5	2	10	5
Wilson	James William	S	17	1			2	1	5	4
Goode	John	S	17	1			3	1	6	5
Smith	Harry	S	17		1		1		4	5
Oagelen	Thomas	S	17	1	1		1		4	10
Phillip	John	S	18	1	1		1		4	10
Dawn	Herbert	S	18	1	2	12			16	Hall
Green	Fred	S	18	1	1		5	2	10	5
Oldershaw	John Harris	S	18	1	1	4		2	9	11
Charlton	Edgar	S	18		2	1		1	4	5
Flack	George Terrell	S	19	1	3		1	1	7	5
Baines	Alfred James	S	19	1	1	2			5	12
Moore	Albert	S	19	1	1	1			4	8
Wilson	William	S	19		2	1			3	3
Henson	Charles Wilfred	S	19	1	4		1		7	6
Samways	Harry	S	19	1	4	1		1	6	5
Dunmore	John Thomas	S	19	1	1		1	2	6	5
Burton	John	S	20	1	1		2	1	6	10
Raynor	Stanley	S	20	1	3		1	1	7	5
Faulconbridge	James	S	20	1	1				3	5
Goode	Thomas William	S	21	1	1		3	1	6	5
Raynor	Frederick	S	21		1	1			3	5
Henson	Samuel Renny	S	21		4				7	6
Wallbank	George	S	21		4	1	1		6	5
Charlton	Albert	S	21		2	1		1	4	5
Flack	James Henry	S	22	1	3		1	1	7	5
Frain	Tom	S	22		1				1	1
Edge	Ralph Thomas	S	22	1	2	12			16	Hall
Housley or Thousley	Joseph	S	22	1	1				3	4

Surname	First names	Marital Status	Age	Couple	Adult M	Adult F	Children M	Children F	Total	Number Rooms
Sibey	Sidney	S	23	1	1			1	4	5
Tuckwood	William	S	23	1	1				3	4
Henson	George Henry	S	23	1	1				3	5
Henson	Harold	S	23	1	4		1		7	6
Murden	Herbert	S	24	1	1				3	5
Woodhouse	Archibald Thomas	S	24		2	1	2		7	5
Powell	Arthur	S	24	1	4	1		1	6	5
Wilkinson	Fred (Frater)	S	25		1	2	1		4	5
Wagstaff	Harry	M	25						2	6
Whitney	Henry	M	26		1	1		1	5	6
Neal	Frederick John	S	27		1	4			7	15
Boyfield	James	S	27	1	2				4	4
Wheatley	Albert	M	27		2				2	7
Wright	William	S	27		1	1			3	3
Frain	William	S	28	1					1	1
Taylor	Percy	M	28		1		1		5	3
Richards	Joseph	S	28		3			2	3	2
Greenham	George	M	28	1					2	2
Henson	Thomas Cecil	S	28	1	4		1		7	6
Porter	Fred	M	28	1		1		1	4	5
Davenport	Joseph	M	28	1					2	3
Burton	John Henry	M	29	1	1		2	1	6	10
Booth	William Edward	M	29	1			1		3	5
Booth	William Edward		29	1	1	3	4		11	5
Mellor	William Street	M	30	1		1	1	1	4	7
Allen	John William	M	30	2		3			9	
Woodhouse	Joseph	M	30	1			1		3	4
Hipwell	John	M	30	1				1	3	4
Woodhouse	John	S	30	1	2	1	2		7	5
Stevenson	Frank	S	30	1	1	2			5	5
Whitney	William	S	30	1	1	1		1	5	6
Headland	Charles	M	30	1				2	4	5

Surname	First names	Marital Status	Age	Couple	Adult M	Adult F	Children M	Children F	Total	Number Rooms
Beardsley	John Henry	M	30	1				1	3	3*
Sibey	George Henry	M	33	1	1		1	1	4	5
Murden	James	M	33	1			1	2	5	5
Boyfield	Thomas	S	33	1	2				4	4
Morley	Samuel	M	33	2	1		2	1	8	9
Sly	Frederick G	S	34	1	1	1			4	3
Smith	James	M	34	1			3	1	6	4
Fletcher	Arthur	M	35	1		1	1	2	6	3
Moore	William	M	35	1			2	3	7	8
Barnes	William Panton	M	35	1			1		3	5
Cooper	Frederick	M	35	1					2	4
Dean	John	M	36	1	1		2	1	6	4
Smith	Jesse Harry	M	36	1				6	8	5
Faulconbridge	Thomas	M	37	1			2	1	5	5
Bradshaw	William	M	37	1	1			2	5	2
Richards	John	S	38		3				3	4
Stevenson	Frank	M	38	1			2		4	4
Stevenson	Samuel	S	39	1	1				3	4
Underwood	Harry Herbert	M	39	1		1			3	7
Thompson	Ernest Montague	M	40	1					2	3
Musgrove	John	M	40	1			1	3	6	3
Simpkin	Edward	M	40	1			1	2	5	3
Burton	John	M	41	1				2	2	5
Jackson	Tom	M	42	1			2	2	6	4
Pinchin	Edward	M	43	1		1	1	2	6	5
Breedon	Charles Edward	M	43	1				2	4	15
Hardy	William Ebenezer	M	43	1	1	4	1		7	5
Flack	Terrell	M	43	1	3		1	1	7	8
Payne	Alfred George	M	43	1		2		1	5	6
Monks	William	M	44	1	1				3	5
Faulconbridge	Joseph	M	44	1	1				3	5
Green	Sam	M	45	1	1		5	2	10	5

Surname	First names	Marital Status	Age	Couple	Adult M	Adult F	Children M	Children F	Total	Number Rooms
Heron	S A	S	45		1	3			4	7
Wilson	George	M	46	1			2	1	5	4
Goode	John	2xM	46	1			3	1	6	5
Eley	George William	M	46	1			3	1	6	3
Tuckwood	William	M	46	1					3	4
Blatherwick	Walter	M	46	1			4	3	9	6
Papworth	Albert Edward	M	47	1			2		4	4
Sullivan	William Maurice	S	47		4	1		1	6	5
Cooper	Charles	S	47		3	1			5	5
Booth	John Henry	M	49	1	1	1	1	1	11	5
Hill	Robert	M	49	1		3			2	4
Gilbert	William	S	49		3	1	1		5	5
Paling	Alfred	M	52	1		2		2	6	6
Horner	William Carrington	M	53	1	1		1		4	10
Henson	Thomas	M	53	1	4		1		7	6
Dunmore	George	M	54	1	1		1		6	5
Murden	John	M	55	1	1				3	5
Edge	Thomas L K	M	55	1	2	12		2	16	Hall
Oldershaw	William	M	55	1	1	4	2	1	9	11
Woodhouse	John	M	58	1	1	1			3	9
Boyfield	John	M	58	2	2				4	4
Allen	James	M	59	1	1	3	1	1	9	7
Henson	George	M	60	1	2	1			3	5
Woodhouse	John	M	61	1	1		2		7	5
Massey	William	M	61	1	1	2			2	6
Stevenson	Charles	M	63	1	1	2			5	6
Richards	John	Widower	64		3				3	2
Parkins	George	M	64	1	1				2	2
Andrew	William	M	66	1	1	2			5	12
Moore	Reuben	M	66	1		1	2		4	8
Pursglove	Samuel Stanley	Widower	66	1	1		2		2	5
Stevenson	Samuel	Widower	67	1	1			1	6	4

Surname	First names	Marital Status	Age	Couple	Household Adult M	Adult F	Children M	Children F	Total	Number Rooms
Raynor	William	M	67	1	1				3	5
Severn	John	Widower	68	1	1			2	5	5
Cooper	John	Widower	68		3	1			5	5
Barker	James	M	69	2	1		1	1	8	9
Goodson	John	S	69	2	1		2	1	8	9
Bradshaw	James	M	74	1	1		2		3	4
Pike	William	M	75						2	3
Ryder	John	M	75	1	1	1			2	4
Faulconbridge	Thomas	M	77	1					2	4
Margetts	William	M	79	1					2	2
Cordon	Samuel	M	82	1					2	5
Stevenson	Thomas	M	84	1					2	3
Stevenson	Samiel	M	86	1	1				3	4

Couple = Married couple
S = Single, M = Married
*1 down 2 up
Names in bold indicate those for whom a military record was found.

Appendix 5: Civilian Rates of Pay in 1914

Average Wage in 1914
For a basic 58 hour week: 16s 9d
This had risen for a 52 hour week to 30s 6d in 1918
Source:British Historical Statistics by B. R. Mitchell

In 1913-1914 the average wage was £1 6s 8d per week or £69 p.a.
Source: 20th Century Britain. Economic, Social and Cultural Change. Edited by, Paul Johnson. Longman, London and New York; 1994, page 6, ISBN 0 582 22817 4 PPR

A sergeant in any of the branches of the armed forces would exceed the average wage in 1914.
The poorest paid private would achieve 45% of the average wage.

Wages
1. Miners
Average wage for a miner in South Wales in 1914 was 9s per day; (x5.5 = £2 9s 6d per week).
Miners worked mostly on piecework.
From their wages would be deducted costs of equipment, time lost for illness or injury.

2. Agriculture
In 1914 a wage of 16s 9d would be paid for a 58 hour week.

3. Building Craftsmen
85d for 10 hours in 1914 i.e. 20s 6d for a 58 hour week.
Sources: www.wirksworth.org.uk
Information taken from the "British Labour Statistics: Historical Abstract 1886-1968"
(Department of Employment and Productivity, 1971.)
and Brown and Hopkins, 1955. (Reference 13 – Bibliography)

Working Hours
At the turn of the century many workers received a half day on Saturday working until 12-00. Others were not so fortunate and agricultural workers could work a full seven days a week depending on the season. Shop workers worked 80-90 hour weeks and domestic servants even longer.
Source: 20th Century Britain. Economic, Social and Cultural Change. Edited by, Paul Johnson. Longman, London and New York; 1994, page 111, ISBN 0 582 22817 4 PPR

Expenditure
Working class people spent 3/4 of their income on food and housing. Expenditure on leisure, except for alcohol, was non-existent for 1/3 of the working class.i 20th Century Britain.
Source: Economic, Social and Cultural Change. Edited by, Paul Johnson. Longman, London and New York; 1994, page 112, ISBN 0 582 22817 4 PPR

Appendix 6: Casualty figures

Great War Casualty Figures

Country	Number Under Arms (Million)	Killed Number (Million)	Killed %	Wounded Number (Million)	Wounded %
Russia	12	1.7	14.17	4.95	41.25
Germany	11	1.77	16.1	4.22	38.36
Britain (Empire)	8.9	.91	10.22	2.09	23.5
France	8.4	1.36	16.19	4.27	50.8
Austria-Hungary	7.8	1.2	15.38	3.62	26.4
Italy	5.6	.65	11.6	.95	16.96
U.S.	4.3	.12	2.8	.2	4.65
Turkey	2.85	.325	11.4	.4	14.04
Bulgaria	1.2	.088	7.33	.15	12.5
Total + Others	52.05	8.123	15.61	21.15	40.63

Source: www.pbs.org/greatwar/

The population of England, Scotland and Wales in 1911 was:
Male   19,754,447
Female   21,076,949
Total   40,831,396
Source http://homepage.ntlworld.com/hitch/gendocs/pop.htlm

Casualty figures of the villages

	Number Under Arms	Killed Number	Killed %	Wounded Number	Wounded %
Roll of Honour book	40	4	10		
Plus those who died immediately after the war		7	17.5	10	25
Plus those of 1911	70	5	7.14		
Plus those who died immediately after the war		8	11.4	21	30
Total				29	41.4

Appendix 7. List of the villagers wounded or damaged in the Great War

Surname	First Names	Regiment	Service Number	Rank	Wounded/Illness
Baines	Alfred James	Royal Fusiliers	75263		Gassed 15 02 1918
Booth	Joseph William	Canadian Overseas Exped. Force	530003	Not found	Discharged as physically unfit
Boyfield	James	Royal Army Service Corps	447991	Private	Yes
Dawn	Herbert	Labour Corps	378186	Private	Sick ('flu) 1918 11 09
Dunmore	John Thomas	Royal Field Artillery	T55861	Private	Slightly wounded, 1915 05 09
Edge	James Vernon	Sherwood Foresters		Lieutenant	Severely wounded, 1915 10 14
Flack	George	Royal Army Medical Corps		Private	Wounded at Vimy Ridge, 1916 05 16
Goode	John	Sherwood Foresters	26755	L/Corporal	Class P wound, discharged 1917 05 05
Goode	Thomas	Sherwood Foresters		Private	Wounded, arm, shoulder, side at Neuvechapelle, 1915 03 10 Hand wound at the Somme Slight neck wound at Lens Severely wounded 1918 08 14
Greenham	George	Sherwood Foresters	201868	Private	Wounded in the head at Gorre
Headland	Charles	Royal Garrison Artillery	31577	Driver	Malaria, 1918 07 26
Henson	George Henry	Sherwood Foresters		Private	Declared 'no longer physically fit for war service' in 1918 04 12
Hudson	Edmund	London Scottish 14th Batt.	86097	Private	Somme, 1916 07 01. Treated for shell shock. Acute bronchitis Discharged 1917 11 24 as no longer fit for military service Died 1919 11 24
Hudson	William	Lincolnshire Regiment	16382	Private	Wounded in the abdomen, Nieppe Forest? 1918 03 00. Deafness of right ear, 1916 08 29
Hughes	Harry Alfred	Royal Army Ordnance Corps	O/24687	Private	Right testis removed, 1918 09 00 Secondary growth removed, 1919 09 00 Grade IV discharge, 1919 06 22 Died 1920 06 22

Surname	First Names	Regiment	Service Number	Rank	Wounded/Illness
Moore	Albert	Sherwood Foresters	117214	Lieut., Capt.	Gassed at Ginchy
Moore	Thomas	Royal Army Service Corps	171689	Private	Gassed at Gorre
Phillip	John	Royal Field Artillery	417026	Gunner	Wounds. Discharged 1918 09 17
Rayner	Stanley	Royal Army Service Corps	36614	Driver	Burned hands 1919 10 07
Raynor	Joseph Frederick	Sherwood Foresters		Private	Wounded in the right shoulder and leg, Lonnebeke 1917 09 266. Severely wounded right arm and left leg. Discharged 1918 04 16
Samways	Harry (S)	Royal Field Artillery	810690	Driver	Sickness, 1918 12 03
Sibey	George Henry	Sherwood Foresters	305162	Private	Discharged 1917 09 13.
Sibey	Sidney	Royal Army Service Corps	TS5190	Shoeing smith	Discharged 1917 02 19
Sly	Frederick	Sherwood Foresters	27997	Private	Sickness. No longer physically fit for war service 1916 12 09
Smith	James	Sherwood Foresters	28913	Private	Discharged on the grounds of 'not likely to become an efficient soldier (on medical grounds)'. 1916 02 24
Stevenson	Frank	Sherwood Foresters	19119	Private	No longer physically fit for war service. 1918 02 10
Wallbank	George	West Riding Regiment	32690	Private	Wounded. Discharged 1918 11 18
Wells	Arthur	Royal Army Service Corps	33710/30710	Private	Nasal Polyps, 1915 05 06
Pauley	Edward	Royal Engineers	241893	Sapper	Discharged, code 392, xvi, sickness, 1917 06 15. Died 1920 03 09

APPENDIX 8. GRADES OF FITNESS IN THE BRITISH ARMY AND THOSE OF THE VILLAGERS WHERE KNOWN

FITNESS GRADES OF CONSCRIPTS IN WW1

A: Fit for active service.
A1:   Fit for overseas duties as regards physical and mental health and training.
A2:   As A1, except for training.
A3:   Returned Expeditionary Force men, ready except physically.
A4:   Men under 19 who would be A1 or A2 when aged 19.

B: Free from serious organic disease, able to stand on lines of communication in France or garrison duties in the tropics.
B1:   Able to march 5 miles, see, shoot with glasses and hear well.
B2:   Able to walk 5 miles, see and hear for ordinary purposes.
B3:   Only suitable for sedentary work.

C: Free from serious diseases, suitable for home service.
C1:   As B1
C2:   As B2
C3:   As B3

D: Unfit, but could be in 6 months.
D1:   Regular RA, RE or infantry command depots.
D2:   Regular RA, RE or infantry regimental depots.
D3:   Men in any depot or unfit awaiting treatment.
www.militarian.com

In WW1 almost half the men conscripted were considered unsuitable.
www.broughttolife.sciencemuseum.org.uk

MEDICAL CLASSIFICATION OF STRELLEY/BILBOROUGH MEN WHERE KNOWN

Boyfield	James	B2
Brewster	Wilfred Charles	A
Dawn	Herbert	B1

Appendix 9. Places served in by the men listed in the Roll of Honour book

Surname	First Name	Date	Age	Enlisted	Served
Appleyard	George	1915 12 08	18	Volunteered	Belgium, France, Somme June 20 1915 to Feb 1918
Appleyard	Henry	1918 09 11	18	Conscripted	North Sea
Booth	John Henry	1914 12 12	17	Volunteered	France. Shot/brought down 7 German aircraft between 1916 07 03 and 1917 04 18
Brewster	Edwin George	1914 09 16	19	Volunteered	France; Ypres, 1915; Somme, 1816; Arras, 1917. Captured 1918 04 27
Brewster	William Charles	1918 04 18	19	Conscripted	Crome
Brewster	William John	1914 12 15	17	Volunteered	
Carlisle	Frederick	b.1896 09 02	19?	Conscripted	
Dale	Cyril	1914 09 26	22	Volunteered	Egypt & Palestine: Senussi, Gaza, Beersheba, Sheria, Jerusalem, Jenin, Tiberius, Damascus
Dobney	George	1915 10 07	17	Volunteered	Egypt & Palestine 1917 06 to 1918 05. Beersheba, El Nuggar (Horse killed beneath him)
					Embarked for France & ship torpedoed, 1918 05 26-27. Transferred to Arras 1918 06 17
Edge	Ralph Thomas	1915 04 25	26	Volunteered	Egypt, Beersheba, Jerusalem and Syria
Edge	James Vernon	1914 10 02	24	Volunteered	France, Hooge
Edge	Roger Francis	1916 08 28	18	Conscripted	Ypres, Cambrai, Arras, Maubeuge and Cologne
Faulconbridge	James	1915 12 15	23	Volunteered	Bellenglise, Ramincourt
Flack	George	1914 09 02	22	Volunteered	Ypres, Vimy Ridge, Somme and Messines Ridge
Flack	William	1914 09 02	18	Volunteered	Egypt and Gallipoli
Garton	Ferdinand	1902 04 26	18	Volunteered	North Sea, Mediterranean, Atlantic and Jutland
Goode	Alvin	1915 12 12	24	Volunteered	
Goode	Thomas	1911 12 11	21	Volunteered	France, Neuvechapelle, Somme, Lens and Cambrai
Goode	William	1915 05 07	20	Volunteered	France, Somme, Arras, Paschendale, Armentieres and Ypres
Greenham	George	1915 11 29	33	Volunteered	France, Somme, Lens, Loos, Bellenglise, Montbrehain and Bohair
Henson	Sidney Scott	1914 12 08	18	Conscripted	Salonika, Egypt and Palestine and France (Bellenglise)
Henson	Charles Wilfred	1918 06 20	26	Volunteered	
Hudson	Edmund	1915 11 24	20	Volunteered	France Vimy Ridge, Somme
Hudson	Robert Atkinson	1914 09 07	25	Volunteered	France, Loos, Ypres, Messines Ridge, Vimy Ridge, Somme, Ypres, Cambrai
Hudson	William	1917 04 00	30	Conscripted	Merveille, Lys Front and Nieppe Forest

105

Surname	First Name	Date	Age	Enlisted	Served
Hughes	Harry Alfred	1916 11 02	36	Conscripted	Mesopotamia, Basra, Baghdad, India, Muttra, Meerut
Jackson	Herbert	1914 12 11	17	Volunteered	France, Armentieres, Monchy Wood, Somme, Vimy Ridge, Arras, Messines Ridge, Boessinghe, Ypres, Cambrai, Noyon
Mann	Cornelius	1915 11 10	22	Volunteered	Arras, Armentieres, Ypres, Peronne, Memin
Mellor	William Street	1916 06 18	35	Conscripted	Merchant Fleet Auxilliary
Moore	Albert	1914 09 00	20	Volunteered	Neuvechapelle, Somme, Ginchy, Arras
Moore	Thomas	1915 08 20	26	Volunteered	Somme, Arras, Ypres, Bellenglise, Gorre
Palin	Alfred John	1914 12 00	19	Volunteered	France
Pearson	Thomas William	1918 06 12	18	Conscripted	Home Service
Pinchin	James Edward	1918 04 11	21	Conscripted	Home Service
Raynor	Joseph Frederick	1916 02 24	26	Volunteered	Ypres, Lonebeke
Shipstone	Joseph Ewart	1918 06 01	21	Conscripted	Ishmala, Palestine on Garrison Duty
Stevenson	Simeon	1918 04 23	20	Conscripted	Home Service
Wells	Arthur	1915 01 14		Volunteered	Egypt Alexandria and Cairo. Salonika
Woodhouse	Joseph	1914 08 04	33	Volunteered	Home Service
Woolcott	Thomas	1914 11 14	18	Volunteered	France & Belgium Arras, Ypres, Jassy

106

Appendix 10. Fitness levels and physical characteristics of recruits from the villages where known

Medical classification of Strelley/Bilborough men where known

Boyfield	James	B2
Brewster	Wilfred Charles	A
Dawn	Herbert	B1

Physical characteristics

Name	Height	Chest (Ex)	Weight	Hair	Eyes	Complexion	Identifiers
Carlisle F. C.	5' 4"	34"					
Dawn H.	5' 6 1/2"	32" (4")		Brown	Blue	Fresh	Appendix scar
Dunmore J. T.	5' 3 1/2"	36" (4")			Grey	Fair	
Green C. W.	5' 9"				Grey		
Green G. E.	5' 6"		158 lb	Brown	Grey		Tattoo, left forearm
Hudson Edmund	5' 8"	38" (3")	138 lb	Dark brown	Brown		
Sibey Sidney	5' 8"	35" (2")					
Smith James	5'	32" (2")		Black/Grey	Blue	Fresh	Scar, left thigh
Stevenson Simeon	5' 8 1/2"	39" (3")					Scar, left forearm
Wilson J. W.	Short	Medium		Brown	Grey	Fresh	
Woodhouse Joseph	5' 8 1/2"	40" (2")		Brown	Brown		

Appendix II. Army Rates of Pay 1914

War Office Instruction 166 (1914). Daily Rates

Royal, Horse, Field and Mountain Artillery

	s	d
Driver	1	2.5
Gunner	1	2.5
Bombardier	2	3
Corporal	2	6
Sergeant	3	2
Second Lieutenant	8(9)	6
Lieutenant	9(10)	6
Captain	15	0

Infantry

Private	1	1
Corporal	1	9
Sergeant	2	6
Second Lieutenant	7	6
Lieutenant	8	6
Captain	12	6

Army Service Corps

Driver/Private	1	2
2nd Corporal	1	9
2nd Corporal (Mechanical Transport)	2	2
Corporal	2	0
Corporal (Mechanical Transport)	2	6
Sergeant	2	7
Sergeant (Mechanical Transport)	3	3
Second Lieutenant	7	6
Lieutenant	8	6
Captain	12	6

Royal Engineers

Second Lieutenant	8	6
Lieutenant	9	6
Captain	13	6
Major	16	0

ROYAL ARMY MEDICAL CORPS

Private	1	2
Corporal	2	1
Sergeant	2	8
Lieutenant	14	0
Captain	15	6

ROYAL FLYING CORPS

Air Mechanic 2nd	2	0
Air Mechanic 1st	4	0
Corporal	5	0
Sergeant	6	0
Flight Sergeant	7	0
Flying Officer	20	6

Source Long, Long Trail.

APPENDIX 12. LIST OF THOSE FOR WHOM MILITARY RECORDS WERE NOT FOUND AND SOME INDICATION AS TO WHY

Surname	First name	Reason
Allen	John William	Multiple choice (222)
Blatherwick	Charles Walter	Not found
Blatherwick	George Thomas	Not found
Booth	Herbert	Multiple choice (167)
Boyfield	Thomas	Not found
Bradshaw	William	Multiple choice (198)
Breedon	Charles Edward	One record: no fit
Burton	John	
Burton	John Henry	Multiple choice (91)
Burton	John	Multiple choice (377)
Burton	William	Multiple choice (399)
Charlton	Albert	Multiple choice (66)
Charlton	Edgar	Multiple choice (19)
Cooper	Frederick	Multiple choice (296)
Davenport	Joseph	Multiple choice (695)
Dean	John	Multiple choice (351)
Dunmore	William	Not found
Faulconbridge	Thomas	Not clear
Faulconbridge	Joseph	Not clear
Flack	Terrell	Multiple choice (7)
Fletcher	Arthur	Multiple choice (325)
Frain	William	Not clear
Frain	Tom	Not clear
Goode	Harry	Multiple choice (48)
Green	Fred	Multiple choice (707)
Green	George E	Not found
Hardy	William Ebenezer	Multiple choice (5)
Henson	Thomas Cecil	Multiple choice (11)
Henson	Harold	Multiple choice (46)
Henson	Samuel Renny	Multiple choice (3)
Hipwell	John (A)	Multiple choice (13)
Housley	Joseph	Multiple choice (11)
Jackson	Tom	Multiple choice (413)
Jackson	Hector	Multiple choice (639)
Monks	William	Multiple choice (56)
Murden	James	One record: no fit
Murden	Herbert	Multiple choice (3)
Musgrove	John	Multiple choice (25)
Neal	Frederick John	Multiple choice (16)
Oagelen	Thomas	Not found

Oldershaw	John Harris	Multiple choice (2) not fit
Papworth	Albert Harold	Multiple choice (11)
Payne	George Alfred	Multiple choice (38)
Pinchin	Edward	Not found
Richards	John	Multiple choice (641)
Richards	Joseph	Multiple choice (447)
Shaw	Robert Arthur Hillary	Multiple choice (57)
Smith	Jesse Harry	Not found
Smith	Harry	Multiple choice (3463)
Stevenson	Samuel	Not found
Stevenson	Frank	Died 1911?
Taylor	Percy	Multiple choice (355)
Tuckwood	William	Multiple choice (5)
Underwood	Harry Herbert	Multiple choice (16)
Wagstaff	Harry	Multiple choice (16)
Wheatley	Albert	Multiple choice (46)
Whitney	William	Multiple choice (29)
Whitney	Henry	Multiple choice (314)
Wilkinson	Fred	Multiple choice (13)
Wilson	William	Multiple choice (116)
Woodhouse	John	Multiple choice (1170)
Woodhouse	Archibald Thomas	Not found
Wright	William	Multiple choice (1471)

Memorial, in Strelley churchyard, to the fallen of the Great War

Fig. 10 Map of Bilborough Parish showing the census route of 1911

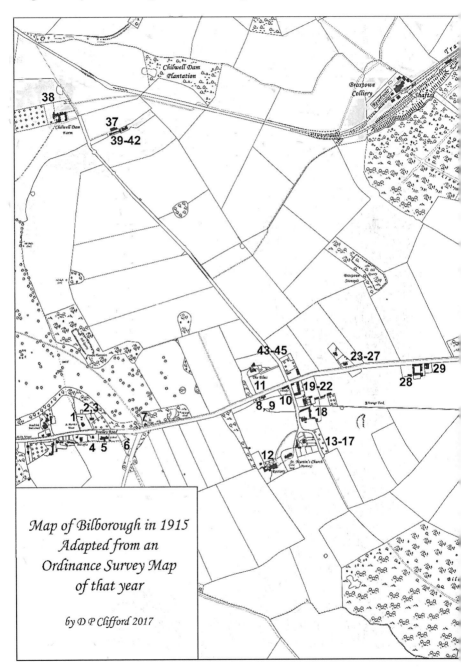

*Map of Bilborough in 1915
Adapted from an
Ordinance Survey Map
of that year*

by D P Clifford 2017

Broxtowe Wood

34-36

Broxtowe Lane

Broxtowe
Hall

33

Broxtowe Lane

32

30, 31

Aspley Lane

Shepherd's Wood

rough Wood

114